THE REALLY PRACTICAL GUIDE TO
NATIONAL CURRICULUM 5–11

David and Wendy Clemson

Stanley Thornes (Publishers) Ltd

First published in 1989 by:
Stanley Thornes (Publishers) Ltd
Old Station Drive
Leckhampton
CHELTENHAM GL53 0DN
England

Reprinted 1990

British Library Cataloguing in Publication Data

Clemson, David
  The really practical guide to National Curriculum 5–11
  1. Great Britain. Primary Schools. Curriculum. Planning
  I. Title   II. Clemson, Wendy
  372.19′0941

  ISBN 0-7487-0056-0

Typeset by Tech-Set, Gateshead, Tyne & Wear.
Printed and bound in Great Britain at The Bath Press, Avon.

Contents

Preface

This book is intended to support debate, discussion and action in primary schools. Our intention is to provide, in a readable and accessible form, a set of items which will enhance the possibility of positive and creative responses to the demands of the National Curriculum.

We want to make it clear that we are not uncritical of the National Curriculum. We do believe that there is *nothing more important than the education of young children*. The legislators and many of those who are implementing this curriculum change are breathtakingly ignorant of primary schools and shamefully patronising of young children. However, we are also aware that regardless of discussion on the merits of the development, it is the case that the teacher in primary school will have to initiate and make operational the demands and requirements of the legislation. We are keen to support positive moves by teachers in this initiation, in their own interests and, more importantly, those of the children in their care.

Teaching in primary schools is intense and demanding work. We think of teachers as always being under pressure and without time to reflect on issues at length. One of the key words we have used in the title page to each section is support. The result is, we hope, a 'hands on' book, jargon-free as far as possible, that you can dip into for inspiration, explanation and example.

Acknowledgements

Thank you to our small daughter Frances, for putting up with us while we were writing this book. She sets the pace, for she writes books and does it much quicker than we do.

The authors and publishers are grateful to the Controller of Her Majesty's Stationery Office for permission to reproduce the extracts on pages 19, 21, 87, 103, 104, 109, 110, 111, 112 and 114.

How to use this book

Section A will provide you with the background to the National Curriculum, explaining why we have a National Curriculum in this form. The middle sections of the book are practical and intended to give direct advice, supported by examples, of ways in which to view the National Curriculum in action. Section E is a self- and school-evaluation workshop which will help you create the right agenda for that action.

▶ If you are not sure where to start, look at Section B (what is in the National Curriculum) and then Section E (using your own strengths and the National Curriculum). Then look at Section A (where the National Curriculum came from and why it is here now). Finally dip into Sections C and D (making the National Curriculum work).

▶ Consult the section title page to find out what the section aims to do.

▶ Read the introduction to a section if you want a frame of reference.

▶ Adapt the examples to fit your situation.

▶ Do not expect this book to have all the answers. Every school, class and teacher is different.

A
BACKGROUND

This section comprises an overview of some of the events and initiatives which led up to the introduction of the National Curriculum. It is not exhaustive, but does 'set the scene' and will support you in:

▶ personal reflection on current educational developments

▶ discussion with colleagues, visitors, parents and governors

▶ the interpretation of articles on education.

Introduction

Whether or not education is a political football or a political issue has been a recurrent theme since King Alfred the Great encouraged a planned education system. In any age it is tempting to state that education is particularly at risk, or exciting, or on the threshold of a new epoch. Whether or not ours is a time of particular historical significance is a matter for the future historian. But for teachers, parents and most importantly children, this is clearly a period of rapid change and intensive activity.

In the European traditions of education, prescribed curricula are not a new phenomenon. Indeed in the last century, prescription by the church and then, increasingly, by the state, created the foundations of the system we have today in the UK. But with the expanded (and diversified) opportunities for all young people, the last 150 years have brought about an increasingly diverse and complex set of alternative views on the aims and purposes of education.

The early teachers and pupil teachers were viewed as instructors and as such could be seen to be operating in close accord with the stated aims and objectives of the ruling classes of the day. When Mr Gradgrind in Dickens' *Hard Times* says, 'Now what I want is Facts . . . Facts alone are wanted in this life,' he is in tune with the generally agreed purpose of schooling of the times. However, as teachers became more educated and access to schools more available for all, then a growing concern for children, their needs, and their learning became more important for many. At the turn of the century many of the interest groups started to differ in their views on the purposes of schools and schooling. No longer was there common and wide agreement on the ways in which children should be taught, nor was there consensus on the subjects, or their facets, which should make up the curriculum.

Why there is a National Curriculum now

In many respects the introduction of the National Curriculum is an attempt to re-establish common understanding, if not agreement, on the aims, purposes and content of state schooling from 5 to 16. The Education Reform Act of 1988 set new legal requirements for the school curriculum and these were introduced in the autumn of 1989.

The National Curriculum has not appeared by accident. Nor has it come about totally by design. Rather it is the offspring of a number of influential individuals, in both the politics and the profession of education, who have been affected by a range of committees, consultants, and journalists. It is a child of mixed parentage, but that does not mean that this child cannot grow, prosper, and be both forward-looking and beneficent. Much of the dynamic of the National Curriculum has been generated in the last 25 years. Many primary teachers are of that generation which was educated post 1944 and trained during the sixties, so the development of the National Curriculum corresponds with their professional lifetime. To develop a working understanding it is necessary to look at the modern history of education.

NATIONAL CURRICULUM ORIGINS

The sixties: growth and diversity

Towards a child-centred approach

The sixties was a period in which there was an educational boom. Management by pupil-teacher ratio was a 'good thing' in that more teachers could be employed with rising rolls. Comprehensive schooling and the gradual disappearance of the 11+ examination underlined the concern with individual expression and growth. The formation of the Schools Council in 1964 with its apparent progressive approach, and the publication of the child-centred Plowden Report (1967) were clear signals of a shift from predominantly content-based curricula to a concern with the process of education. Whether the popular image of the progressive primary school was borne out in reality is debatable. There is evidence to suggest that change within schools was actually very gradual and that many teachers responded to 'progressivism' by accommodation and the blending of approaches. However, among the public at large and politicians there was a sense of rapid change. The perceptions of some were that the changes, real or apparent, were not welcome.

A swing away from progressivism

Following the expansion of higher education, the increase in length of teacher-training courses, and the emergence of the B.Ed. as a professional qualification, there was a move towards much closer examination of the effectiveness of educational provision.

No single event was the catalyst for the switch from uncritical expansion to detailed monitoring and evaluation. It is as though there was a growing collective consciousness that some important questions needed to be asked about both the quality of state education and the content of curricula in state schools. However, there were some notable influences.

It was in 1969 that the contributors to the Black Papers provoked a wide range of reactions to their view that progressive primary education and comprehensive secondary education were 'bad things'. Concerns were expressed particularly about 'standards'.

The seventies: accountability

Standards come in for criticism

Immediately after the sixties expansion there followed half a decade which was characterised by a plethora of critical reports, comments and newspaper articles. Many of these said that money had been thrown uncritically at the 'problem' of state education and that 'standards' had fallen, or been abandoned. The publication of the Bullock Report in 1975 confirmed some people's concerns about a lack of the 'basic skills'. It is no coincidence that the year before publication the DES set up its Assessment of Performance Unit; a unit which is now having a quiet but real influence on the development of the National Curriculum. The mid-1970s was the watershed when apparently unfettered growth and proliferation of educational practices came in for close scrutiny. The age of accountability was upon us. Public attention was particularly focused on primary practice in the mid-seventies.

The William Tyndale affair

A major socio-political and educational row broke out about the practices in the William Tyndale Junior School, Islington. Massive media coverage, dramatic interventions, claims and counter-claims amongst professional educators, and ultimately formal legal disputes, ensured the place of William Tyndale in history of education texts. There was a huge public scandal about the way in which some of the staff of the school seemed to have forsaken the 'basics' in an attempt to cultivate a radical form of schooling. Officials were chastised and some teachers were removed. The outcome of the affair indicated that teachers actually had limited control over the shape and nature of the curriculum.

The Yellow Book and the start of the great debate

In the midst of all of the speculation on primary education as a whole, and in response to the many loud voices in both 'traditional' and 'progressive' camps, the then Prime Minister, James Callaghan, asked the Secretary of State for Education for a memorandum to clarify the areas of real public concern. Fred Mulley produced this supposedly confidential memorandum, known as the Yellow Book, and it led to banner headlines immediately. Leaks of material from the DES have not always been noted for their impact as front page news, so this indicates how strong were the influences and pressures then being brought to bear on the Government. Bennett with his *Teaching Styles and Pupil Progress* (1976) gave opportunities for headlines of the type, 'Formal Teaching is Best', and it is therefore no surprise that Callaghan highlighted national concerns, and initiated Government response. This important development has come to be known as the Great Educational Debate. The context set for that debate more than ten years ago is very familiar to all in education today: curriculum 5–16, assessment of standards, teacher training and education, and schools and the world of work.

Key events and trends in the seventies

1 Black Papers
2 Assessment of Performance Unit set-up
3 Bullock Report: 'A Language for Life'
4 William Tyndale affair
5 Bennett's *Teaching Styles and Pupil Progress*
6 Launch of the Great Debate on Education

The eighties: increased central control

Educational reform

The move from expansion through criticism to reconstruction has culminated in increased central decision-making about the school curriculum. The Education Reform Bill (1988) contains important requirements for the organisation and management of schools, their governance, and their relationships with the community. The introduction of the National Curriculum coincides with such matters as opting out, local financial management, and staff appraisal. The Bill draws on a number of developments in the early eighties, all of which were underpinned by a concern for the education system to serve the needs of the economy. Whatever our views on this apparently utilitarian approach, it has increased the effectiveness of some teachers. One of the first of the initiatives in the eighties was in the field of youth training.

TVEI

'Relevance' and 'value for money' might be seen to be the buzz words of this decade. In the early eighties a connection was made between a lack of appropriate training for youngsters and subsequent unemployment. A natural outcome of this connection was criticism of secondary education. Schools were accused of having failed the nation by not equipping young people for jobs. Education was seen to be in need of reform in order to arrest and reverse the perceived decline in British industry. The Technical Vocational Education Initiative (TVEI) was launched in 1982 and supported by the Manpower Services Commission, not the DES. Despite this implied criticism of the DES Keith Joseph, then Secretary of State for Education, gave support to the initiative. Schools were drawn into TVEI provision and many of the 14–16 age range were provided with TVEI-influenced curricula.

The move to what is now dubbed an enterprise culture has percolated into the primary sector. What is particularly interesting for primary teachers is the familiarity they have with the language of TVEI teaching methods and curricula. Problem-solving approaches, topic work, and the development of information and study skills, are known areas in the primary school. This territory was well charted in Galton's Observational Research and Classroom Learning Evaluation (ORACLE) project which was published in 1980. ORACLE provided an alternative view to that of Bennett in 1976.

Changing views on teaching style

Galton and his colleagues grouped the primary teachers in their survey into four main styles: individual monitors, class enquirers, group instructors, and style changers. The ORACLE team did not place a value on style in the way that earlier research had done. They were concerned to survey practice. Half of the teachers in the study were deemed style changers of one sort or another. It would seem that most teachers were adapting their practices in answer to children's responses and the need for varied stimulation. However, the context in which Galton's work had been undertaken was rapidly altering.

For some years there had been a changing role for HMIs and they had moved into an advisory capacity. But in the early eighties greater emphasis was again given to the inspectorial nature of their job. This was brought about by a requirement to make public their reports on schools and other educational establishments, making the performance and practice of teachers open to public scrutiny. Whilst the effects of this accountability may not be growing uniformity of practice, there is no doubt a need to examine the effects of inspection on teaching styles. This is not to say that the ORACLE work is no longer valid, but it is important to recognise that public accountability may give undue emphasis to 'approved' teaching styles and that teachers may respond to this pressure rather more than they have before. It is our view that the ORACLE work can offer much to schools implementing the National Curriculum.

Primary teacher training and CATE

Growing accountability through the eighties has not been confined to schools. The supply of teachers to the profession has also been the subject of close scrutiny and the Committee for the Accreditation of Teacher Education (CATE) laid down course criteria that affect all prospective primary teachers. The main criteria are that all primary B.Ed. students must study a subject at their own level for 50 per cent of their course. This includes application of that subject to the primary classroom. All students must also have a minimum of 100 hours of formal work on mathematics and language. To this must now be added 100 hours science and design and technology. These new criteria are currently in the consultation stage. They clearly map onto the National

Curriculum requirements for primary schools. The nature of training, the quality and characteristics of students, and the relationship between schools and training institutions over the next few years will be of great importance to National Curriculum delivery.

Primary schools and the micro

Before leaving the eighties which would appear to be characterised by greater public accountability, increased specification of content, and increased responsibilities for headteachers and their staffs, it is necessary to note what may, with hindsight, become a much more important influence on the educational system: the introduction of the micro.

Through the Micro-electronics Education Programme (MEP), and subsequently the Micro-electronics Education Support Unit (MESU) there has been a growing availability of micro-computers and associated software. In the early days, the initiatives were hardware led and so seen as limited and limiting in many primary schools. However, there is now an appreciation of the need for good software which supports learning and is not a substitute for the teacher. Additionally the possibilities brought about through word processing, desk-top publishing, and the use of databases and spreadsheets have started to be realised in many primary schools. These initiatives will grow, and they will have an undoubted impact on the knowledge and skills content of the National Curriculum. It is no accident that the statutory orders so far produced for mathematics and science are on loose-leaf paper and in ring-back folders.

Key events and trends in the eighties

1 Youth training and the MSC
2 ORACLE project
3 HMI reports
4 CATE criteria
5 Education Reform Bill
6 Information technology

The nineties and beyond

Crystal ball gazing is not a safe activity in education. With the benefit of hindsight, it is possible to see the inevitability of the introduction of a National Curriculum. Ten years ago it was hard to predict this development. However, it is possible to judge probabilities, and the evidence to hand indicates that there are going to be clear changes for schools, teachers and children. The rate of change in any particular area is impossible to determine, but we have no doubt that our predictions are reasonable and will become evident over time. Not all of the changes may work in the best interests of children. However, forewarned is forearmed, and, with inspired planning, we can maximise the effects that we see as beneficial. The major developments likely in primary schools have to do with changing demands on teachers, meeting children's learning needs, and assessment arrangements.

Changing demands on teachers

The role of headteachers   No longer will there be a chance for message taking and consultation by and for staff during lesson time. Children's time on task is more important. Thus headteachers will strive to maximise communication outside lesson time, achieve whole school planning, and engage staff as a team in a joint enterprise. All of this will result in the redefinition of the role of headteacher as co-ordinator.

Teamwork within and between schools   Teaching teams (led by curriculum-area leaders) will look for ancillary and administrative assistance to support their professional activity. Resourcing of this help may mean that teams decide to forgo automatic replacement of full-time teachers!

In order to provide the expertise, to share good practice, and enhance resources provisions, many schools will federate with neighbouring schools. The effect of this on the profession would be to change some of the skills needed by teachers and lead to more open attitudes to skill sharing.

The outcome of increased teamwork, additional ancillary staff, and federated schools will lead to a new definition of career teaching. Headteacher posts will become co-ordinating jobs supported by financial and administrative personnel. Career teachers might take a route which leads not to Head but to team leader. A school with a manager and a teaching leader, teacher teams and a group of support staff sounds a radical form of organisation compared with schools of the past, and so it would be. But whatever form of organisation emerges, it must serve the best interests of all children.

INSET   To help them respond to the National Curriculum in the first instance teachers are receiving some in-service training opportunities. It is crucial that the impetus be maintained if the profession is going to make the positive possibilities of the National Curriculum a reality and maintain good practice. To do this teachers will need regular and continuing INSET throughout their career. Voluntary attendance at courses will change to a requirement. Much as teachers do in the USA, teachers here will have to undertake validated in-service courses and produce evidence of their having done so. Much of this in-service will take place outside normal school hours or terms. New contracts of employment will come, as will new styles of partnership with INSET providers. In many cases this will also mean a new relationship with initial teacher education, so that the development of teachers will be seen as being shared both prior to and in service. Some schools may become training schools affiliated to and run in collaboration with initial teacher-education institutions.

Staff appraisal   From 1989 there is to be formal staff appraisal of all teachers. To have the opportunity to formally engage in a review of your experience and future needs means that you can be creative in developing new strengths and roles, which should be to your advantage. Only if staff appraisal were to be used to label poor teachers would there be regression. Experiences in other sectors of employment indicate that after initial fears and confusions, it is possible to make annual staff appraisal a positive and formative process.

Groupings of children and their learning needs

Flexible grouping   In line with the development of teamwork will come a move towards more varied patterns of groupings of children. Whilst schools may continue year or family groupings for pastoral and overall administrative purposes, there will be much more movement across years, rooms and content than is common today. Children's needs in relation to the National Curriculum will mean that consideration must be given to the best way of offering appropriate experiences. By this we are not suggesting the adoption of a subject timetable with movement of children to subject teachers; rather we are suggesting that many of the skills and concepts across the curriculum will have to be delivered across the school. This will put the emphasis on learning opportunities rather than teaching structures. It will also mean that schools are going to have to teach children how to become independent and self-confident learners, who will be active in deciding their own learning needs.

Resource-based learning   In order to sustain learning at the appropriate levels for each individual child, there will be a review of teacher deployment in relation to learning opportunities. An increase in the use of resource-based learning is one likely outcome. This means more use of information technology. The development of learning packages including software, books, and activities for which resources are available in the school or community will become important.

Assessment arrangements

Continuity and progression   The development and wide use of profiles for primary age pupils is a likely response to the demands for records and assessment of children's progress through the National Curriculum. Records of personal achievement and profiles will go forward through the sectors of formal education and beyond into employment. To bring this about there will have to be a greater exchange of personnel, information, and resources between different sectors. There has been, in many localities, a growing appreciation of the need for feeder schools to engage with the secondary school. It will now be necessary for all schools to initiate development plans which blur the traditional distinctions between schools. This may not herald the return of the middle school or the all-through school, but it will make the jobs of primary and secondary teachers less distinct. The methods, aspects of content, and skills development will be shared more in order to grapple with the National Curriculum from year R to year 10.

Moderation   The other major innovation which will bear on assessments is moderation of schools by other schools. For many years it has been common practice in higher education for tutors from one institution to formally moderate the curriculum and standards of another institution. There has been an increased use of teachers in such roles with the development of GCSE. Moderation of primary school curricula and assessments by visiting teachers will become an accepted duty over the next decade.

Predictions for the nineties and beyond

1 Changing role of the headteacher
2 Teamwork and flexible staffing
3 Compulsory INSET and teacher appraisal
4 Increased range of groupings and resources for children's learning
5 Consistent profiles and records across all years of schooling
6 Moderation across schools

NATIONAL CURRICULUM GUIDE

This section is about the National Curriculum documents themselves: getting into them, interpreting them and using them. The aims are to give support in:

- ▶ understanding the National Curriculum documents
- ▶ coping with the breadth of learning envisaged
- ▶ approaching topic work.

Introduction

The National Curriculum documents are rather daunting. Of necessity they are lengthy and densely worded, and the content and breadth of coverage are hard to assimilate at one go. Their presentation and layout, while internally consistent, do not make them accessible at a glance.

Educational standards

In order to be familiar with the needs and requirements of the National Curriculum it is important to know something about standards.

The National Curriculum has been devised in an attempt to respond to concern about standards. For some teachers this is highly contentious for they would claim that, in important ways, standards have not declined. We do not intend to consider the merits of the arguments here, but it is useful to be clear that the issue of standards has been under discussion for some long while.

For example, in 1862 Robert Lowe, the Education Minister, issued the Revised Code which introduced payment by results. It led to better attendance at school (teachers only being paid per pupil), improvement in school organisation and a preoccupation with the 'basics'. A new balance point was established between church and state in schooling provision. However, the resulting curriculum was narrow, and high and low attaining pupils were neglected. 'Standards' were established in the three Rs. For example, Standard V in Reading was achieved by reading some poetry aloud from a reading book in use with children in the first class in the school. Compare this with the range of expectations in, say, level 3 of the National Curriculum English (reading). Clearly expectations are much greater today than 130 years ago, but some of the pressures might appear to be the same and the dangers are evident. Teachers may feel that they have to teach to externally determined targets and that they must teach the same thing to the whole class at the same time, and in the same order. The effect of this is a lessening in provision for the high and low attaining pupils. However, these need not be the consequences of the National Curriculum if teachers are enabled to fully exploit the knowledge that has been garnered on learning and teaching since Lowe boasted of his new system: 'If it is not cheap, it shall be efficient; if it is not efficient, it shall be cheap.'

What kind of curriculum is the National Curriculum?

There are many ways in which the curriculum can be looked at and analysed. These include process models, problem-solving approaches, and in terms of areas of knowledge and experience. The National Curriculum is presented under subject headings. Subject labels are a shorthand used to indicate the existence of a set of related concepts and skills which, when acquired, allow you to view the world through a particular and distinctive pair of spectacles. Geographers may view a landscape in particular ways, while historians and biologists would view the same landscape in related but different ways.

Making the National Curriculum work: subjects and topics

To locate the National Curriculum in the pattern and expectation of the work done in the primary school, we will focus on the curriculum in action through the use of subjects and topics. Thematic and topic work can be seen as a problem-solving or issues-based approach to the curriculum.

While we make a strong case for topic work, we do know that topic work alone is not enough. With creative planning many teachers can already foresee ways in which the children can be engaged in lively cross-curricular study which will meet many of the requirements of the National Curriculum. Not all National Curriculum requirements can be met in this way. There needs to be subject work too. Subject and topic work, flexibly managed, will meet the National Curriculum demands.

The planners of the National Curriculum do recognise that the relationships between subjects and the processes of learning cannot be described only in subject terms. In the documents, the opportunities for children to learn in one curriculum area, and through that experience add to their knowledge in another area are now explicit. It is also in the teacher's own interests to consider such cross-curricular work wherever possible. The more areas the children can make progress in at the same time, the better. There is recognition that effective delivery of the National Curriculum depends on you being flexible and far-sighted, and defining the curriculum in terms of both subjects and topics.

To get a handle on the opportunities and potential of the National Curriculum it is important to understand the jargon, and to be able to analyse and articulate both through the curriculum and across the curriculum provision. The chapters in this section are designed to help you do this.

CHAPTER 2

UNDERSTANDING THE DOCUMENTS

A teacher's route to knowing and then implementing what is in the National Curriculum documents depends on an understanding of two things: the people and organisations involved in National Curriculum production, and the jargon used in the documents.

People and organisations behind the documents

There are a few key groups and organisations which have contributed to the compilation of the National Curriculum. Knowledge of the jobs these groups do actually allows us to predict the emphasis of their output, and modify prejudices about them. We have 'named' some of the people behind the documentation, for we feel that, as classteachers, you may often sense you have little power and do all the work. You may sometimes feel 'put upon', and that people who have qualifications, interests and experience outside education are setting the pace. To put the record straight, we have outlined some of the past and current educational involvement of the National Curriculum VIPs.

SEAC and NCC

To bring about the educational changes the National Curriculum Council (NCC) and the Schools Examinations and Assessment Council (SEAC) were created. The NCC advises on the whole curriculum, the SEAC on modes of assessment and how results are recorded and reported. Both Councils advise on information dissemination. The Secretary of State set up working groups to make proposals about the content of subjects. NCC is a consultative group which makes recommendations regarding these to the Secretary of State. The proposals are then converted to draft orders, subject to further consultation and then, with parliamentary approval, become legally binding requirements.

The Secretary of State who personally championed the National Curriculum and overviewed it was Mr Kenneth Baker. He may have relied heavily on others' advice regarding the detailed proposals. He is Oxbridge educated and an experienced parliamentarian.

The Chairman of the National Curriculum Council is Mr Duncan Graham. He was Chief Executive of Humberside County Council and former Chief Education Officer for Suffolk. In addition to other management posts in the education service he taught for six years in Glasgow schools.

The Chairman of the Schools Examinations and Assessment Council is Mr Philip Halsey, Deputy Secretary at the Department of Education and Science since 1982 and a one time headmaster.

APU and TGAT

The Assessment of Performance Unit (APU) is a DES group which has been in existence since the early seventies. It is concerned with surveying children's performance in a range of subjects but particularly language, mathematics and science. It has surveyed children, usually at ages 11, 13 and 15. Whilst its findings have been useful to teachers in helping to identify areas of strength and weakness in children's performance, it has never had a clear influence on educational policy. However, it will have affected the views of testing embraced in the Education Reform Bill, and it will make a real contribution to the development of assessment by SEAC.

The Task Group on Assessment and Testing (TGAT) was set up by the Secretary of State in July 1987 to advise on assessment and testing within the National Curriculum. A report was published in December 1987 discussing the principles behind the assessments, assessments in practice, the phasing of their implementation and the support system (INSET) needed. This and three supplementary reports published in March 1988 comprise the work of the TGAT.

When this Group was convened Professor P.J. Black, Professor of Science Education, University of London since 1976 and Head of the Centre for Educational Studies, Kings College, London since 1985, was appointed Chairman.

Working groups

The Secretary of State set up Working Groups to start the planning of the foundation subject areas. They were to recommend the content of the programmes of study and attainment targets. The Groups started to work in a phased sequence, so that the results of their efforts could be implemented in phase. At the time of writing, documentation is available following the work of the English, Mathematics and Science Working Groups. All Working Groups comprised the following sorts of people: teachers, lecturers, inspectors, professors, researchers, consultants and advisers.

All Working Groups consulted the following sorts of organisations and people: professional associations, advisers' associations, agencies and organisations connected with education, assessment and validating bodies, careers associations, industry, local education authorities, parents, post-16 further and higher education institutions and staff, primary education organisations, religious bodies, special educational needs organisations, and subject bodies.

When the English Working Group was formed, Professor Brian Cox, Professor of English Literature and Pro-Vice Chancellor of Manchester University, was appointed Chairman.

Mr Duncan Graham took over as Chairman of the Mathematics Working Group in January 1988. (See the note on him under NCC above.)

Professor Jeff Thompson, one time school teacher, then Professor of Education and Pro-Vice Chancellor of Bath University, was made Chairman of the Science Working Group.

The National Curriculum jargon

It is vital to know the words being assigned special meanings in the context of the National Curriculum. How do these meanings differ, if at all, from the conventional ones?

Most of the things labelled in the National Curriculum are in wide use in schools. Teachers have long worked out what it is the children in their care should learn; they have had aims and objectives for the children, and recognised that individuals have differing amounts of competence in specific learning areas. All these can be matched to the jargon of the National Curriculum; the programmes of study, profile components, attainment targets and levels, etc.

What is important to remember now is that aspects of the curriculum have been rigorously defined, and must be taken on board by all teachers. Figure 2.1 is a chart showing the key National Curriculum words, and where they fit into the pattern of teaching and learning. We have put these words into context for each of the three core subjects in Figure 2.2.

Figure 2.1   National Curriculum key words: where they fit into a pattern of teaching and learning

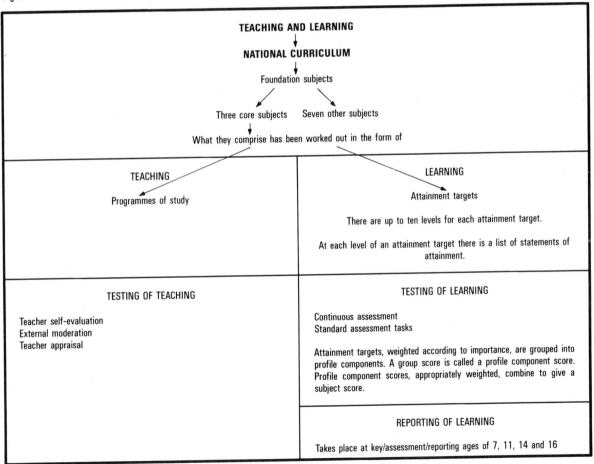

15

Figure 2.2 The core subjects in primary schools (key stages 1 and 2)

SUBJECT	TEACHING	LEARNING		TESTING/REPORTING
		ATTAINMENT TARGETS	LEVELS	
E N G L I S H	Set out in programmes of study, key stages 1 and 2.	5ATs: (profile component 1) AT1 speaking and listening (profile component 2) AT2 reading (profile component 3) AT3 writing, AT4 spelling and AT5 handwriting	ATs 1, 2, 3 have ten levels; ATs 4, 5 may have fewer: 1–3 (key stage 1), 2–5 (key stage 2)	Continuous assessment through the years and across the curriculum SATs at 7 and 11 ATs grouped for assessment and reporting into three profile components. To compile profile component 3 score apply these weightings to the ATs: writing 80%, spelling 20%, handwriting 10%. All PCs then carry equal weighting at key stages 1 and 2.
M A T H E M A T I C S	Set out in programmes of study, level by level. Profile components weighted as follows for planning: PC1 (ATs 1–8) 60%; PC2 (ATs 9–14) 40%.	14ATs: (profile component 1: knowledge, skills, understanding and use of number, algebra and measures) AT1 using and applying mathematics, AT2, AT3 and AT4 number, AT5 number/algebra, AT6 and AT7 algebra, AT8 measures (profile component 2: knowledge, skills, understanding and use of shape and space and data handling) AT9 using and applying mathematics, AT10 and AT11 shape and space, AT12, AT13 and AT14 handling data.	All ATs have ten levels, except AT6 (starts at level 2) and AT7 (starts at level 4): 1–3 (key stage 1), 2–6 (key stage 2)	Continuous assessment through the years SATs at 7 and 11 ATs grouped for assessment and reporting into two profile components: ATs 1–8, ATs 9–14. Weightings are under consideration.
S C I E N C E	Set out in programmes of study, key stages 1 and 2. Profile components weighted as follows for planning: key stage 1 PC1 (AT1) 50%; PC2 (ATs 2–6; and ATs 9–16) 50%; key stage 2 PC1 (AT1) 45%; PC2 (ATs 2–6) and ATs 9–16) 55%.	14ATs (1–6 and 9–16): (profile component 1: exploration of science, communication and the application of knowledge and understanding) AT1 exploration of science (profile component 2: knowledge and understanding of science, communication and the applications and implications of science) AT2 the variety of life, AT3 processes of life, AT4 genetics and evolution, AT5 human influences on the earth, AT6 types and uses of materials, AT9 earth and atmosphere, AT10 forces, AT11 electricity and magnetism, AT12 the scientific aspects of information technology including micro-electronics, AT13 energy, AT14 sound and music, AT15 using light and electro-magnetic radiation, AT16 the earth in space.	All ATs have ten levels, except AT7, AT8 and AT17 which start at level 4, but need not be studied at key stage 2: 1–3 (key stage 1) 2–5 (key stage 2)	Continuous assessment through the years SATs at 7 and 11 ATs grouped for assessment and reporting into two profile components: AT1, ATs 2–6, 9–16. Weightings are under consideration.

Finally we have made a National Curriculum jargon list. The list is not exhaustive. It includes all the words we needed to define when reading the official documents. The definitions are, as far as possible, in everyday words, and brief. Inevitably a little of the meaning is sometimes lost. The list is intended as a reminder rather than a dictionary and the jargon should be put back in context to understand it fully.

Assessment criteria	Devised by teachers or determined by SATs; used by teachers to decide what level children have reached in the goals set for learning (ATs)
Attainment target (AT)	Learning goal in a foundation subject, made up of up to ten levels
Basic curriculum	Foundation subjects plus religious education
Continuous assessment	Assessment within school (internal) over the whole year, done by teacher, using various methods and contexts
Core subjects	English, mathematics and science
Education Reform Act 1988	An Act of Parliament which, in its sections on compulsory schooling, applies to children in England and Wales. It was passed in 1988 and makes many amendments to the law relating to education, but most importantly requires all children of compulsory school age to pursue the same basic curriculum, known as the National Curriculum.
Formative	Test plus assessment results are formative when used to improve teaching and learning and show what a child needs to do next.
Foundation subjects	Three core: English, mathematics and science, and seven others: technology, history, geography, music, art, and physical education; (and for secondary children, a modern foreign language)
Key stage	There are four of these; they are the periods of schooling up to 7, 7–11, 11–14, 14 to the end of compulsory education.
Level of attainment	Attainment targets are broken down into these; they are cumulative, but the levels reached by a child will vary from one target to another, according to talent. There are up to ten levels for each attainment target.
National Curriculum (NC)	What's to be taught (PofS), and learning goals (ATs) for core and other foundation subjects, and the assessment arrangements
National Curriculum development plan	School plan of changes needed, for example in curriculum and staffing, and what needs to be done, to carry through the changes to meet the National Curriculum requirements
Principle of access	For each learning goal (AT), what's to be taught (PofS) provides access to levels reflecting the entire ability range.
Profile component	Attainment targets are grouped in these for assessment and reporting.
Programmes of study (PofS)	What's to be taught in each subject in order to reach learning goals (ATs)

17

Reliable	Reliable assessment methods give the same result for similar performances.
Reporting ages	Also called key or assessment ages; they are 7, 11, 14, 16, when formal reported assessment occurs.
Standard assessment task (SAT)	Devised by TGAT to test children at key (reporting) ages; results will supplement continuous assessment.
Statement of attainment	A list of these corresponds to each learning goal (AT).
Statutory order	Allows additions to and updating of the Education Reform Act
Summative	Test and assessment results are summative when used to tell parents of their child's progress.
Teacher assessment (TA)	Assessment by teachers
Ten point scale	List of ten levels, each corresponding to a year of compulsory schooling
Valid	Valid assessment methods measure what they are intended to measure.
Weighting	Weighting occurs for reporting and assessment when some ATs are given a bigger percentage of the whole which makes up the profile component. Profile components can, if appropriate, be weighted when they are put together to make an overall subject score. Weighting is applied to the profile components for planning purposes in order to achieve balance within each subject.
Whole curriculum	Foundation subjects, religious education and other things taught

CHAPTER 3

TEACHING THROUGH SUBJECTS

Subjects: the common language for curriculum description

Almost everyone over the age of five can name a school subject. Labels such as English, history, and art are frequently used in curriculum discussion. The use of such labels has been common since the introduction of formal schooling. For example. in the *Handbook of Suggestions for the Consideration of Teachers and Others Concerned in the Work of Public Elementary Schools*, published in 1905, the curriculum was described as being:

> **❝** *English, Arithmetic, Religious Instruction, History, Geography, Nature Study, PT, Art, Craft (Boys), Needlework (Girls), Music.* **❞**

Apart from the boy/girl distinction in crafts, the expansion of arithmetic to mathematics, and nature study to science, this list is very similar to that of the National Curriculum.

Subjects in the National Curriculum

The subjects the National Curriculum prescribes are **three core subjects:** English, mathematics, science; and **seven other foundation subjects** (six for key stages 1 and 2): technology (including design), history, geography, music, art, physical education, (and a modern foreign language for key stages 3 and 4, 11–16). These subjects, along with religious education, comprise the statutory minimum scope of the curriculum. But:

> **❝** *The foundation subjects are certainly not a complete curriculum.* **❞**
>
> DES, *National Curriculum: from Policy to Practice* (HMSO, 1989) para. 3.8

According to the advice given in this DES booklet, the whole curriculum, for children at key stages 1 and 2, will include health education. A number of cross-curricular learning areas are also identified. Those of relevance to young children are: economic awareness, political and international understanding and environmental education.

Why subjects?

The National Curriculum has been conceived as it has, partly because a subject-labelled curriculum is accessible, understandable, and perhaps, more acceptable to the man or woman in the street. However, it is as well to remember that subject labels are artificial tags that we give to areas of knowledge and experience. Subjects are not whole, discrete and immutable. Even more importantly, what we assign a subject label to is not the same for all of us. Share with colleagues what mathematics is, and part of their definitions will be the same while part of them will be different, according to the individual's past experience, current skills, vision, etc.

What the National Curriculum does is set down, under subject headings, a series of annotated lists which increase in content complexity over time. The lists are arranged in levels, and, like building blocks, are cumulative, sitting one on the other. The annotated lists are to be implemented by all teachers. In other words, there is to be an enforced common understanding about what each subject comprises. Though the levels become more and more complex, as they build up, it is the first levels which are the most important, for it is on these that the others rest.

Because of the familiarity of subjects, you probably do not view subject teaching with unease. However, the expectations regarding subject learning are extensive. Planning has to be detailed if delivery is to be effective.

Putting the subjects into action

In the official documents there are some examples of activities and problems the children might tackle, but apart from these, there are no clues about all the things you have to do to translate the programmes of study into action and achieve the attainment targets. They do not tell you *how* to plan and teach the curriculum. We will make some general points about planning and then take each core subject in turn, making some detailed suggestions about how to teach it. You will, of course, be planning for the other subjects which make up the whole school curriculum, alongside the core subjects. Strategies that you find work for you and your class in the core subjects may then be useful in implementing National Curriculum directives in the other foundation subjects.

Our suggestions regarding planning and teaching in the core subjects are based on these beliefs:

> ► Though subjects are not discrete, and do overlap, they are different in ways that affect planning, teaching and assessment.

> ► A single sweep through the substantive attainment targets in a school year may be inappropriate; teachers' plans need to take account of the following:
> Children may forget by June what they learn in January;
> Children mature socially over the year and may therefore tackle their learning differently at one end of the year from how they do at the other;
> Children develop intellectually as a result of all their learning, so that, for example, work in science may support later understanding in mathematics.

> ► There is too little time to tackle teaching and learning for individual children; even children in a small class need group planning.

Curriculum balance

The role of language

Language work has a special and unique place in the primary curriculum.

> 66 *In the primary school, opportunities to develop children's competence in listening, speaking, reading and writing arise in all aspects of the curriculum.* 99
>
> DES, *English for Ages 5–11* Proposals of the Secretary of State for Education and Science and Secretary of State for Wales, (HMSO, November 1988) para. 2, 7, p. 7

Language can be seen, then, not only as an essential core subject but as the vehicle for all intellectual development, for thought and the demonstration of thinking. Putting it another way, the quality of the language experience you give your class will profoundly affect their thinking skills.

English or Welsh is the very fabric of our education, so, in determining what balance of activities should be available to children in school we see language work as being pivotal. We would argue that detailed evaluation of your language work and the development of a broad and balanced language programme is the best way of ensuring your awareness of the curriculum as a whole. Whilst subject groupings, session times and resource management are all important factors in offering and maintaining curriculum balance, language is the mortar that binds the curriculum together. In the discussion of teaching strategies for the core subjects we will therefore treat English differently from the others.

Time

Now that teachers have been told what subjects to teach, the next issue to tackle is that of how much time should be spent on each subject. However:

> 66 *there are not centrally prescribed time allocations for particular subjects, and the ERA expressly prevents their being set out in Orders . . .* 99
>
> DES, *National Curriculum: from Policy to Practice* para. 4.3

There are some assumptions made concerning the curriculum balance required for children to be able to reach the appropriate levels in the attainment targets. Headteachers and classteachers can be helped by the NCC's recommended weightings given to aspects of subjects.

> 66 *. . . in drawing up their schemes of work for mathematics and science, schools should be guided by the weightings recommended by NCC, in considering the relative importance in the curriculum of the aspects to which the weightings relate.* 99
>
> The Education Reform Act 1988: National Curriculum, Mathematics and Science Orders under Section 4, DES Circular, no. 6/89, VII, 41

For key stages 1 and 2, the weightings are listed in the circular just quoted as follows:

	Key stage 1	Key stage 2
Science	%	
Exploration of science	50	45
Knowledge and understanding of science	50	55
Mathematics		
Knowledge, skills, understanding and use of number, algebra and measures	60	60
Shape and space and data handling	40	40

In relation to schemes of work and planning there seems to be no mention of weightings for the profile components in English. For reporting and assessment purposes they all have equal weighting.

Foundation subjects

To ensure balance all foundation subjects need to be appropriately planned. The earlier availability of detailed documentation concerning core subjects does make it tempting to plan for those subjects in detail, and then see what time and resources are left for the other foundation subjects. If you plan this way the risk is that there will not be much time left, and certainly not enough! It is true that some of the work in the foundation subjects can be covered using the topic work approach discussed in Chapter 4, but you will still need to plan subject-specific work in these subjects too. A way of achieving balance across the curriculum may be to group the subjects, so we have worked out some possible groupings to help you or your department or school develop your own shared framework for subjects or areas of knowledge and experience. These are shown in Figure 3.1. The groupings are for expediency and are not exhaustive. In our experience a primary school day is usually cut into three or four sessions, so we have suggested the number of selections to be made from each subject group to fill four sessions.

Hints on planning for all core subjects

1   Find out what levels the children have reached in the attainment targets and how well each child is equipped to tackle the next steps by looking at internal records *across the curriculum*.
2   Next, work out what pre-task skills the children need for the next phase. For example, what reading skills do they need and what technical vocabulary? What thinking and problem-solving skills do they require? Note that, for example, the skills necessary for mathematics are not just mathematical skills!
3   Fill the skills gap *now*, with remediation.

Figure 3.1 Some possible ways of grouping school subjects: 5 to 11

GROUPING 1		
LANGUAGE FACILITY	CULTURAL UNDERSTANDING	LOGICAL SKILLS
Language of mathematics Language of science English for mathematics English for science English	History Geography Religious education Environmental studies Music Art Drama	Mathematics Science Technology (including design) Physical education Health education
In a four-session day, children do one activity from the language facility group, one from the cultural understanding group and two from logical skills.		

GROUPING 2				
MATHEMATICS	SCIENCE	LANGUAGE	EXPRESSIVE ARTS	SOCIAL AND MORAL STUDIES
Mathematics	Science Technology (including design) Geography Physical education Health education Environmental studies	English	Music Art Drama	History Religious education
In a four-session day, children do one activity from each of four groups. The selection is varied over a week, so that in five days the children have done activities in each of the five groups four times.				

GROUPING 3				
HUMANITIES	SCIENCES	LANGUAGES	ARTS	MATHEMATICS
History Geography Religious education Environmental studies	Science Technology (including design) Health Physical education	English	Music Art Drama	Mathematics
If this grouping is implemented, children work in a two-day cycle, on day 1 doing work in two of the subject groups (for example, humanities and science) and on day 2 doing work in the remaining three subject groups.				

4 Work out a teaching and learning framework for the period of time the children are in your care for each core subject, a school year if possible, a term at a time, if not.

5 Devise an activity list related to the programmes of study and to meet the appropriate range of levels within each attainment target.

English

If English is 'all the time and everywhere' in school, you need firstly to look carefully at the programmes of study. These say what must be taught. The next step is to tease out in what contexts these things are best taught, whether in formal 'chalk and talk' lessons, in individual or small group work, or in drama, topic work, history, mathematics, etc. Then your planning must ensure the contexts are made available to all the children so that they work at the appropriate levels in the attainment targets. English has to be planned in at least as much detail as everything else in the curriculum.

As you cannot be working on performance and potential in all ATs at the same time, consider timetabling your focus of attention. You may choose to concentrate on teaching and learning related to one of the profile components at a time, that is speaking and listening, reading or writing. They could be covered in a three-week cycle, in week 1 the emphasis being on speaking and listening, in week 2 on reading, and in week 3 on writing, and so on.

Because language is about communicating you could focus the teaching and learning still further, by looking at the child's language skills and the 'output' – the communication – separately. Figure 3.2 suggests ways of doing this.

Figure 3.2   English: a suggested way of focusing on skills for teaching and learning

SPEAKING AND LISTENING	
CHILD Listening skills Articulacy	AUDIENCE/CONTEXT Speaking appropriately in terms of audience and context
READING	
CHILD 'Mechanical' skills – extracting meaning from print Intellectual skills Memory Listening to the written word Concentration	AUDIENCE/CONTEXT Reading for own pleasure Reading for information Reading to enhance or formulate opinions Reading to support speaking and writing Reading aloud to a variety of audiences
WRITING	
CHILD Understanding and implementation of grammar Spelling skills Dexterity and fine hand control	AUDIENCE/CONTEXT Writing for a range of audiences and contexts (authorship)

Targets and levels   In English there are five attainment targets at key stages 1 and 2. They are:

> AT1 Speaking and listening
> AT2 Reading
> AT3 Writing
> AT4 Spelling
> AT5 Handwriting.

These are grouped into three profile components; speaking and listening AT1, reading AT2, and writing ATs 3, 4, and 5.

Teaching strategies

If you are inclined to use, or required to organise, sessions called 'English' on the timetable, you could plan for all the children to work across the language spectrum every day. In some classrooms it has been common for teacher or child to check that they have done reading, writing and mathematics every day. Add speaking and listening to the reading and writing, and there will be a tick for 'English'.

Speaking and listening   Whatever your timetable looks like in the area of language, the children must be enabled to speak and listen to a range of different audiences (varying in size and composition) in a variety of contexts, and for a variety of purposes. They will include one-to-one conversations with their classmates, older children, teachers and other adults; group discussions in small and then larger groups, with other children, with and without a teacher present; and public speaking to their own class, other classes and the department or school, for example in assembly, and to an invited public audience, for example at plays and concerts. They also need to learn to use tape recorders and computers for communication purposes.

Speaking and listening skills often develop together. That is the assumption made by the compilers of National Curriculum English. It may, however, be useful to you to sometimes focus on either speaking or listening. For example, if you are 'chairing' a group discussion, when the emphasis that day is on speaking, you may note who speaks out confidently and often, and who is reticent. You would also note the competence with which the children speak. Most importantly, with speaking as the focus, you would ensure that everyone had the chance to speak, and your own contributions to the discussion would be in the areas of, for example, encouragement, spoken grammar, colloquialisms and standard English, and vocabulary extension.

Placing speaking and listening at the core of the curriculum does give these skills their proper importance. However, school has not always been a place for talking. The emphasis for the teacher has often been on getting the children to stop talking, to listen a lot, but only to the teacher. In order to meet National Curriculum criteria you will have to allow more child talk and discussion than may have been the case previously. But this talk will have to be constructive and not 'idle chatter', at least not in lesson time. In generating talk in your classroom you will have to determine what talk is constructive, necessary to the purpose at hand and educative. This will mean that both you and the children will need to identify and avoid talk which is distracting. The key to this evaluation of talk is the involvement of the children for it is only through their growing ability to recognise the qualities and characteristics of different kinds of talk that you can genuinely claim to be teaching speaking and listening.

In our experience, the less formality there is about classroom management, the more talk there is, of both the constructive and diversionary kinds. If you feel most at ease with a quiet classroom, you need to plan for three things. The first is clearly identified sessions in which children speak and listen to each other as well as to you. Secondly, a strategy for discussion which will prevent a 'free-for-all'. For example, in a class unused to discussion sessions begin with a five-minute slot at the end of a session. To a listening(!) class explain the strategy: 'I am going to ask you to talk to your neighbour about the question of (dog licences, bedtimes, pocket money, or whatever). I shall give you a minute. I want you to talk quietly, so that only your friend can hear. After a minute I shall stop you and tell you what to do next.' You might stop this first session with a show of hands (for or against dog licences, for example). Through the school year, you can then gradually increase the length of time and size of grouping in discussions. The third planning need is in respect of your own listening development. We all suffer from the anxiety of silence. We ask questions and answer them if there is not an immediate response from the children. We need to learn to wait, and then to really hear what is said. This means curbing our tendency to reinforce the desired answer and lose the opportunity for novel responses or answers which would allow teaching to happen in ways we have not predicted.

Reading   All primary teachers need to be teachers of reading. Though most children eventually learn to read, many still need help with skills development towards the end of their primary schooling. In any case, learning to read does not stop when you have achieved fluency.

Some mix of the following, and other activities of your own devising, will feature in that part of English we call reading:

▶ 'Group' reading of flash cards, captions, and from multiple copies of the same book

▶ Reading aloud for instructional purposes, individually to a teacher, parent, older (more fluent) child and to a bigger audience

▶ Reading: for pleasure
            for information retrieval
            for review purposes ('Find out what it's about. Is it good?')
            in order to form and express opinions
            in order to interpret and analyse

▶ Reading silently for pleasure and information retrieval.

As with all other areas of the curriculum we must look not only at curriculum content, but at the quality of the children's reading experience. Though reading two pages of a reading scheme book to a volunteer helper every day for a week may certainly be ticked as reading, and may be confidence building for some children, it may actually deter others, whatever their reading skills or academic potential. A guide to the quality of experience is the purpose for which it is done. That purpose must have more to do with getting knowledge or pleasure than a tick on a reading list!

Writing   Writing seems a bit easier for teachers to plan for and implement. That may be because the way it is treated in the National Curriculum reflects much of what good teachers have been doing already.

The children must have the opportunity to understand English (or Welsh) grammar, to learn correct spelling, to master handwriting and to write for a range of audiences and contexts, using word processors etc. where appropriate. Lessons that concentrate exclusively on technique and ignore content and context are, on the whole, sterile. In our experience, children seem to find it difficult to transfer learning done in this way. When the weekly spelling tests were abandoned in favour of a displayed word list that the children consulted as and when they needed to, their spelling improved (even after the list was eventually removed). Put grammar and spelling into context. Check both in each child's work, on a regular basis, and discuss errors, possible improvements and progress with each child individually. Though you should have sight of all their written output, don't attempt a detailed analysis on every piece of rough work. The children won't fully understand your comments without some explanation and you won't have time to explain everything to all of them.

There's one final and very important point to make about writing standards. That is that teachers' writing must be as neat and legible as they expect the children's to be, and spelling and grammar must be correct. This applies as much to the comment on a piece of work as it does to the hall display. It is a good discipline to periodically write prose or poetry at the same times as the children and expose your efforts to their critical gaze!

Mathematics and science

Labels we have assigned to teaching strategies

We have worked out a number of possible ways of tackling mathematics and science teaching. They are called *linear* when only one AT or statement of attainment is tackled at a time. Within the linear category, *by the book* refers to a strategy where the order the ATs are tackled in is the same as that listed in the official documents, and *optimal path* means where the teacher picks and chooses statements of attainment from one attainment target at one level, to create a learning pathway for some of the children in his or her care. The strategy is called *combined* when two or more ATs are tackled at the same time. Within the combined strategies there is a *two-strand* approach which sets out a two-part learning programe, the two parts going ahead side by side, and finally the *modular* approach in which ATs are grouped and treated in a thematic way.

We have laboured the point about tackling several levels simultaneously, whatever your strategy, but there's no way of avoiding that (short of changing school organisation, which may take time!)

Mathematics

There are many ways of approaching mathematics teaching and learning. In some ways, both by tradition, and in the way it has been set down in the National Curriculum, mathematics lends itself to a more linear attack than the other core subjects. However, just as subjects are not discrete, neither are attainment targets. Tackling them one by one, at each level, in number order is not necessarily the best way for every child, group or class to learn. The targets are knowledge item lists, and take little account of the processes of teaching and learning. It may be that in the light of experience, you will want to jiggle them around and devise an optimal learning path for the children in your class.

Targets and levels   In mathematics there are 14 ATs. A year-group class will contain children working at a range of three to four levels. ATs 1, 9, 12, 13 and 14 are skills-based. There are nine substantive ATs (AT6 starts at level 2, AT7 starts at level 4). It is predicted that levels 1–3 will be common at key stage 1, and levels 2–6 at key stage 2.

Teaching strategies: linear

By the book   At each level appropriate for the children in the class work on AT2, AT3, AT4, AT5, AT6, AT7, AT8, AT10, AT11, straight through. Check that exercises are built into the work done to meet the appropriate levels in the skills ATs, that is AT1, AT9, AT12, AT13, AT14.

Optimal path   At each level appropriate for the children in the class, work out the sequence in which statements of attainment should be tackled, one at a time. Children may, group by group, do work to satisfy a statement of attainment for one attainment target and then work towards a statement of attainment for another attainment target. The path taken by the children will vary according to what you, in the light of your experience, see as the next step for them.

As an example of this strategy the following have been worked out in Figure 3.3:

> Level 1 – ATs 2–5, 8 and 10–11
> Level 2 – ATs 2–6, 8 and 10–11
> Level 3 – ATs 2–6, 8 and 10–11.

The example presented represents the level range expected in many infant classes. You may need to run all three levels in tandem, taking a statement of attainment at each level at a time. For example, the appropriate sections of the class may be engaged, at the same time, on work leading to:

> AT2 statement 1: (count, read, write numbers to 10) level 1
> AT6 statement 1: (use of symbol for unknown number) level 2
> AT5 statement 1: (explain and predict number patterns) level 3.

Some statements of attainment will take longer to master than others, so the pace of the children will vary. It will also be necessary to ensure that exercises are built into the work done to meet the appropriate levels of the skills attainment targets; that is AT1, AT9, AT12, AT13 and AT14.

Teaching strategies: combined

The two-strand approach   At each level appropriate for the children in your class run a 'two-pronged' mathematics course, the two parts being in process during the same week or so, but not in the same session.

Part A	Part B
AT1 and AT2	AT1 and AT8
AT1 and AT3	AT9 and AT10
AT1 and AT4	AT9 and AT11
AT1 and AT5	AT9 and AT12
AT1 and AT6	AT9 and AT13
AT1 and AT7	AT9 and AT14

28

Figure 3.3 Mathematics: an example of a linear optimal path teaching strategy for levels 1, 2 and 3 (N.B. S = statement)

LEVEL 1	LEVEL 2	LEVEL 3
AT2 S1 Count, read, write numbers to 10	AT6 S1 Use of symbol for an unknown number	AT5 S1 Explain and predict number patterns
AT5 S1 Copy, continue and devise patterns of objects or numbers	AT3 S1 + − facts to 10	AT3 S1 Know and use + and − facts to 20 (and zero)
AT4 S1 Estimate to 10	AT3 S2 Compare two numbers and find the difference	AT5 S2 Mental calculations to 99
AT2 S2 Conserve number	AT5 S1 Explore and use patterns in + − facts to 10	AT6 S1 Inputs/outputs from simple machines
AT8 S1 Compare and order objects without measuring	AT2 S1 Numbers to 100, know tens digit indicates number of 10s	AT10 S1 Sort 2D/3D shapes and explain methods of sorting
AT3 S1 + − to 10	AT2 S2 Half and quarter	AT2 S1 Numbers to 1000 and place value
AT10 S1 Sort 2D/3D shapes	AT4 S1 Estimate to 20	AT4 S1 Know importance of first digit to tell number size. Approximation
AT11 S1 Position vocabulary, such as 'on', 'inside', 'under', etc.	AT10 S1 Recognise some 2D/3D shapes and describe them	AT3 S2 ×/÷/ money problems using calculator as necessary
AT10 S2 Build with 3D shapes, draw 2D shapes, describe them	AT8 S1 Use non-standard measures	AT3 S3 × facts to 5 × 5; 2, 5, 10 times tables
AT11 S2 Give and understand instructions for moving along a line	AT8 S2 Use coins	AT5 S3 Recognise whole numbers ÷ by 2, 5 and 10
	AT3 S3 Whole number + − problems including money	AT11 S1 Reflective symmetry in 2D/3D shapes
	AT8 S3 Know common units in length, capacity, weight and time	AT4 S2 Remainders, know whether to round up or down
	AT5 S2 Odd and even	AT2 S2 Decimal notation of money
	AT11 S1 Angle	AT8 S1 Use wide range of metric units
	AT10 S2 Right-angled corners in 2D/3D shapes	AT8 S1 Choose and use units and instruments
	AT11 S2 Give/understand instructions for turning through right angles	AT8 S3 Estimate using familiar units
	AT11 S3 Types of movement: straight, turning and flip and appropriate vocabulary	AT11 S2 Eight points of compass, concepts of clockwise and anti-clockwise
		AT2 S3 Understand negative whole numbers

29

Note the skills ATs have been set alongisde substantive ATs in parts of this strategy.

Putting this strategy into practice: if, for example, some children are working at level 4, they may in a half term or so of their mathematics lessons tackle:

AT1　Select materials and mathematics for a task; plan methodically

　　　Record findings and present appropriately

　　　Use examples to test statements or definitions

AT3　Multiplication up to 10 × 10

　　　Mental arithmetic + −　two 2-digit numbers
　　　　　　　　　　　　 +　several 1-digit numbers

　　　Using recording　+ −　two 3-digit numbers
　　　　　　　　　　　 ×　a 2-digit number by a 1-digit number
　　　　　　　　　　　 ÷　a 2-digit number by a 1-digit number

　　　Problems　　　　+ −　to two decimal places
　　　　　　　　　　　 × ÷　whole numbers

AT9　(as AT1 using shape problems)

AT10　Understand and use 'angle' vocabulary

　　　Construct two- and three-dimensional shapes.

The modular approach　At each level appropriate for the children in your class run a mathematics modular course. In the autumn term, which is longer than the others, tackle substantive modules called:

Number　AT2, AT3, AT4
Algebra　AT5, AT6, AT7
Measures　AT8
Shape and space　AT10, AT11.

In the spring term do skills modules:

Using and applying mathematics　AT1, AT9
Handling data　AT12, AT13, AT14.

This is, then, a practical/problem-solving term in mathematics.

In the summer term cover remediation and revision. When all ATs are done do complex problem-solving and mathematics investigations across the attainment targets. When children can do all the work at a level, within a module, they should be enabled to work on the next level.

Mathematics plans and outcomes

Whether you use one of the strategies we have suggested for teaching mathematics, or devise one of your own, you will also need to work out a succinct way of setting out mathematics plans and the outcomes of learning. Here is a list of things to consider:

Mathematics AT(s) and level(s)
Resources
Practical work
Reinforcement in other subjects or contexts, and games
Recording of learning by children
Teacher's records of children's learning.

AT3 level 1 has been set out as an example in Figure 3.4.

Figure 3.4 Mathematics: plan and record sheet for AT3 level 1

MATHEMATICS AT3 NUMBER LEVEL 1 + − to 10			
RESOURCES	10 blocks, 10 toys, 10 pencils, 10 children, 10 books, etc. Children make resources: 10 playdough buns (for the baker's shop) 10 'Aunt Sallys' (to take away) Marble runs to create and add scores 10 speckled frogs to take away 10 apples to put on 2 trees, 10 buttons for 2 coats (or more), etc.		
PRACTICAL WORK	Add together 2 sets of blocks, toys, children, etc. to make numbers to 10. Add several small sets to make numbers to 10. Take away from a set of blocks, pencils etc. not exceeding 10. Introduce vocabulary and signs.		
REINFORCEMENT AND GAMES	On flashcards, die, unifix, spinners, etc – the signs and vocabulary. AT4 estimation. Addition and subtraction games made up like bingo and snap.		
CHILDREN'S RECORDING	Picture recording; draw, colour, use of numbers, arrows, boxes, linear sums, vocabulary. Formal addition and subtraction.		
TEACHER'S RECORDS (ONE FOR EACH CHILD IN GROUP)	Addition without recording to 10 Addition with some recording to 10 Subtraction without recording to 10 Subtraction with some recording to 10 Formal addition to 10 Formal subtraction to 10	Introduced	Practised	Mastered

Science

The National Curriculum gives to science more time and emphasis than it has ever had in primary schools. This may be advantageous to the business economy of the future, and give children a new breadth of learning and challenge, but planning, timetabling and resource management are problematic. When looking at teaching strategies in the core subjects, we have labelled them linear and combined. We have said that, to some extent, mathematics can be treated in a linear fashion. The most appropriate strategy for science seems to us to be a mixed linear (through ATs) and combined (across ATs) one.

31

Targets and levels   There are 17 ATs in science, 14 of which comprise the science curriculum for primary schools. AT7, AT8 and AT17 start at level 4 but need not be studied in key stage 2. For the remaining 14 ATs levels 1–3 are the common ones expected at key stage 1 and levels 2–6 at key stage 2. AT1 is skills-based. The other 13 ATs are substantive.

Teaching strategies: linear

By the book   At each level appropriate for the children in your class work through AT2 to AT16 in numerical order. Check that the work actually done meets the appropriate levels in AT1 skills.

Optimal path   Choose an attainment target and work out a teaching plan. This may be of two types:

a) *At one level.* For a group of children devise learning experiences to meet the statements of attainment at their level, for example, science AT14, sound and music, level 5. (See Figure 3.5.)

b) *Across levels.* For groups or the class devise interlocking experiences for the children to meet statements of attainment at several levels, for example, science AT14, sound and music, levels 1, 2 and 3. (See Figure 3.6.)

Teaching strategies: mixed linear and combined

Some ATs can be grouped together more satisfactorily than others. For key stages 1 and 2 the following groupings are suggested: AT2, AT3, AT4, and some aspects of AT13; AT9 and AT16. The other ATs look as though they stand better alone. They are AT5, AT6, AT10, AT11, AT12, AT14, AT15.

Some themes are easier to carry through at some times of the year than at others, for example, it may be easier to work on the life ATs 2, 3, 4 and parts of 13 in the spring term when new life and the growth of plants is much in evidence.

We have worked out a timing programme for the attainment targets, grouping them where appropriate and pinpointing the school term in which they may work best. The choice is yours, but an infant or junior department or primary school which chooses to plan so that the whole department or school is working on the same elements of the programmes of study and ATs (at the appropriate levels) at the same time, will have the advantage of a department/school focus for learning. Resources must be shared, of course, but learning experiences at, say, level 4 can be made available to all the children in the school who need them. Learning outcomes, displays, books, drama, and presentations are then accessible, topical and relevant to all the children in the department or school.

Figure 3.5   Science: optimal path teaching plan at a level (AT14 level 5)

SCIENCE   AT14   LEVEL 5   SOUND AND MUSIC
STATEMENTS OF ATTAINMENT Pupils should: ● understand that the frequency of a vibrating source affects the pitch of the sound it produces ● understand the relationship between the loudness of a sound and the amplitude of vibration of the source ● understand the importance of noise control in the environment.
PROGRAMME OF STUDY ELEMENTS Workings of the ear, kinds of sounds, musical notes, noise in the environment; pitch, loudess and timbre etc. and the way they change according to, for example, the length, tension, thickness and material of a vibrating object; exploitation of change in sound according to the way it is caused, for example, over-blowing.
SOME SUGGESTED ACTIVITIES/EXPERIMENTS Look at/discuss model of ear in section; draw and label Compare ears of other living creatures, hearing aids and mechanical 'sound collectors' Discuss fragility/care to be taken of ears Classify range of sounds Noise – when and where acceptable Sound vocabulary, pitch, loudness and vibration, etc. Explore musical instruments, group according to sound made Make or use homemade and conventional instruments to find out what changes pitch, loudness, etc.

Figure 3.6   Science: optimal path teaching plan across levels (AT14 levels 1, 2 and 3)

SCIENCE AT14 SOUND AND MUSIC		
LEVEL 1	LEVEL 2	LEVEL 3
STATEMENTS OF ATTAINMENT		
Pupils should: ● know that sounds can be made in a variety of ways	● know that sounds are heard when the sound reaches the ear ● be able to explain how musical sounds are produced in simple musical instruments	● know that sounds are produced by vibrating objects and can travel through different materials ● be able to give a simple explanation of the way in which sound is generated and can travel through different materials.
PROGRAMME OF STUDY ELEMENTS Range of sounds, causes and uses; ways of making sounds, including vocalising, striking, plucking, shaking, scraping and blowing using objects and instruments from different cultures. Sorting of sounds and instruments.		
SOME SUGGESTED ACTIVITIES/EXPERIMENTS		
Discuss what sound is and how it is made Make sounds with voice, slapping, stamping, tapping, banging, using elastic bands, strings, sticks and bottles, etc. Look at, discuss and explore sounds from school instruments, and homemade shakers, etc. Listen for other sounds close by and far away; from living creatures and made mechanically Sounds vocabulary	Model of ear, look at and discuss workings of the ear, care of ears and hearing Discover and explain how sounds made in school and on homemade instruments; also on borrowed instruments from other cultures Sort range of sounds/music/noise Extend sounds vocabulary	Discuss and draw ear in section diagram. Write about workings of the ear. Introduction to the orchestra. Group instruments according to how sound is made. Record findings about how sound is made and travels. Noise and the law. Use tape recorder to test and estimate noise levels, and record range of sounds.

A suggested order for science work in the school year

Autumn term

AT6	Types and uses of materials
AT11	Electricity and magnetism
AT12	The scientific aspects of information technology including micro-electronics
AT14	Sound and music

and a first stab at:

AT9	Earth and atmosphere
AT16	Earth in space

Spring term

AT2, AT3, AT4 and parts of AT13 together   Variety of life
                                            Processes of life
                                            Genetics and evolution
                                            Energy (in part)

Spring/summer term

AT5	Human influences on earth

Summer term

A second stab at:

AT9	Earth and atmosphere
AT16	Earth in space
AT10	Forces
AT15	Using light & electromagnetic radiation
AT13	Energy (in part)

Summary

In this chapter we have concentrated on the core subjects. Our intention in doing this is to support you in the initial stages of implementation where priority will be given to English, Welsh, mathematics and science. The remaining foundation subjects will be built, in terms of presentation and organisation, on the blueprint created for the core subjects.

The major points to remember are these:

▶ It is important that the programmes of study are the teacher's first point of reference. Teaching to the statements of attainment would result in a 'paring down' of learning which is undesirable.

► It will be necessary to plan the groupings of subjects and define whole school progression.

► The full potential of the children will not be realised if the National Curriculum is implemented through narrow subject timetabling. The connections between subjects need to be explored and made clear to the children through action.

► An appreciation of the centrality of language in the whole curriculum will characterise good practice.

CHAPTER 4

TEACHING THROUGH TOPICS

Across-subject learning

Traditionally, topic work has been seen as an opportunity to pursue interests or knowledge that are not readily described in subject terms. Perhaps more importantly, it has presented teacher and children with the chance to blur subject distinctions and try to think in novel ways about the information at hand. For example, the topic of North American Indians has been used to enable work which may be labelled geography, history, music, English, art, etc. but the children's thinking and recording has demonstrated learning, which, if it must have a label, would be called environmental education, history of art, etc. There is no doubt that topic work such as this will continue under the National Curriculum. But the often intuitive approach adopted by many teachers and the independent topic which has no planned relationship with subsequent work in other classes will have to disappear. Teachers will need to be sure that what the children are given to do is quite specifically work that addresses the programmes of study and attainment targets.

Why do topics?

Topic work is not being squeezed out of the primary school timetable. On the contrary, a more powerful case can be made for topic work in schools, now that the National Curriculum is here. The reasons for doing topic work are:

Time   It may be difficult to fit in all the work required of both children and teacher without using cross-curricular approaches for some of the time. Through topic work that is carefully planned, the children can be tackling aspects of several attainment targets at one and the same time. The teacher can consequently carry out continuous assessment of the children's progress across a skills and knowledge spectrum, saving time in record compilation.

Applying knowledge   The teacher has the opportunity, while topic work is in progress, to observe whether a child has assimilated knowledge to the extent that it can be applied to new situations in other areas of learning or subjects. Repetition of, for example, a mathematics concept, in increasingly complex and broader settings will allow teachers to observe when the concept can be reapplied within mathematics. Only topic work allows observation of wider application of that concept.

36

Skills   The programmes of study spell out an approach to learning which is not only about what the children should have the chance to learn, but also include the skills they should master. These aspects include, for example, communication skills, reporting and recording, getting information, using resources, making decisions. They are study skills. The children are learning how to learn. The opportunities to do this are often greatest in topic work.

Choosing a working title for a topic

Members of National Curriculum working groups demonstrate in their reporting their keenness that present good practice should not be quashed. We think good practice in topic work happens where it is properly planned and where the teacher is ready to follow up children's ideas during the topic. The topic is not labelled in a way that makes the teacher didactic and children passive.

In one sense you can call the topic what you like. 'Railways' may provoke thinking and planning just as much as: Why does our town have a mainline station? What does the first train out carry and where does it go? 'Just the ticket' – start with a collection of tickets.

Whole-school planning does make it tempting to look for catch-alls like 'The Victorians'. The topic could then be sliced up so that, for example, Y1 do food, Y2 schooling, Y3 costume, Y4 railways and Y5 industrial development.

Another way of approaching the plan may go like this: We aim as a school this term to get the children working on ATs in English, ATs in mathematics and ATs in science (in each case list which ones). We also want the children to learn about: 'Then and now'; their heritage; why the town looks as it does. Each member of staff starts with a different Victorian postcard or photograph of the town. There may be one of the town hall, main street, railway station, shops, gardens, etc.

The postcard or photograph is the class clue in a treasure hunt. The treasure is understanding, related to the programmes of study and attainment targets that the teacher has decided upon. The trail is learning skills, and the method is discovery. Of course the teacher will influence, even decide, the direction the trail takes; but her or his 'idea map' must include, 'What do the children want to know next? What questions are they asking?'

Topic work and group sizes

Topic work does not have to be done by everyone in a class, year group, department or school at the same time. If the planning is done to dovetail topic activities into others, a few children can be doing topic work while others work in subject areas. Topic work for some and subject work for others may give more flexibility to aspects of classroom management. Research has shown that teaching that is done using a variety of groupings, from whole class to small groups, does much to further the development of individual children.

There are advantages in allowing part of a class to work on a topic. The topic group's work, which may be extensive and wide ranging, can be carefully scrutinised by the teacher, as part of the assessment process. To avoid the impossible burden of assessment of every piece of learning done by every child in the class, the teacher can focus especially on the work of the topic groups, while it is in progress. Once that work and the teacher's assessments are completed, it can be the 'turn' of another section of the class, whose work will then receive the teacher's detailed scrutiny. A group or groups of children can do topic work by turns. Each child then receives more teacher time and attention for some sessions, and the teacher has the advantage of a focus for her or his assessments.

Once the topic group's work is planned, some of these ideas and activities can be put into use with the rest of the class, too. It can be done without breaking their subject-based work pattern. For example, physical education can still be done with the whole class, using the topic ideas as a stimulus.

The children working on the topic produce resources for others in the class to use, for example, books, photographs, drawings and models. These topic resources may be used with future groups or classes in other ways. If successful, the topic can be added to a 'topic bank', and then be repeated or modified for future use.

Steps in planning a topic

1   Decide for which children the work is to be planned, and how they are to be grouped.
2   Pinpoint the timing in the school year.
3   Establish a working title.
4   Identify the elements of the programmes of study and attainment targets on which the work will focus.
5   Redefine the topic title, if necessary.
6   Choose a stimulus word or phrase for the heart of the topic web and draw up the web.
7   Check that the web supports the aims identified in 4 above, and if not change the title.
8   Work out assessment and evaluation strategies.
9   Write the planned work into the timetable.
10 Implement and monitor.

Topic webs as planning devices

All topic work relies heavily on the interpretation of the planner. Topic plans with the same title, produced by two different people, may have little in common. When setting out aims, the items selected from the programmes of study and the associated attainment targets will vary from one planner to another. Topic work is 'open' for the teacher and the children. The only limits are those set by programmes of study and attainment targets and within these constraints there is still a great deal of room for the creativity and imagination, of both the teacher and the child. Plans are commonly portrayed through topic webs, examples of which appear later in this chapter. Topic webs are characterised by the following features:

▶   They are idiosyncratic, and reflect the knowledge of the teacher, the resources available and the teacher's predictions about the children's interests.

- ▶ Links between concepts and ideas in the web can be added to incorporate the children's thinking and ideas as much as the teacher's.

- ▶ The web is not exhaustive.

- ▶ The web does not have to be 'exhausted'; if a strand is not working well, the teacher can discard it and take another line.

Some examples of topic work planning

In presenting these examples, we have set out to show:

- ▶ how topic work can fit in with the programmes of study and attainment targets

- ▶ a range of topic names, from specific questions to broad titles

- ▶ the use of topics with a range of group sizes

- ▶ the use of topics with children with a range of ability levels.

It is beyond the scope of this book to present a comprehensive range of topics. The plans developed here are intended to provide frameworks for the exploration of ideas and groupings appropriate to your school. The examples we have given are suitable for the age and ability range recommended. However, this does not mean that they cannot be used successfully with other sizes of group, or children of other ages and abilities.

T1 is for some children within a class or department, working to the same level. This topic plan has been set out in detail, to indicate the kind of planning involved where 'mixed' subject and topic learning is taking place.

T2 focuses on a class or classes, working at a key or reporting age, in this case, top juniors (Y6).

T3 targets an infant class, and is suitable for R, Y1, Y2 or some mix of these year groups.

T4 is for a junior class, and therefore work suitable for Y3, Y4.

T5 identifies a theme which children throughout a primary school may embark on.

Topic plan T1

Age of children and groupings   Two groups of children in a Y3 class (1st year juniors), in all about 10–12 children. For this topic work, they have been ability grouped and are all working at level 3.

Timing   This topic could be done at any time in the school year.

Working title   'What's so funny?'

Aims To work on some of the elements of the programme of study in English. These may include, for example, recounting stories, responding to poetry, role play, discussion, reading poems and books, producing class books, shaping, structuring and planning writing.

The work in English will mean that the children can achieve some of the requirements of the English attainment targets 1–5 at level 3. For example:

> Relating real events to a group
> Following precise instructions
> Listening with concentration to other children
> Discussing stories and poems
> Selecting information
> Writing a complex story
> Shaping a narrative
> Spelling less common words important to the learning context.

Work in English should predominate as the topic is language-based. The children will also work in the foundation subjects: technology, history, geography, music, art, physical education. Work in mathematics and science will go ahead in whole class subject sessions.

Topic web The topic title, 'What's so funny?', needs no refinement, so the next step is to create a topic web, with the title as the stimulus phrase in the middle. The topic web is shown in Figure 4.1.

If much of what is suggested by the web was done by the children, they would not only have met the aims of the teacher, in regard to work on English attainment targets 1–5, but would also have worked on the following:

> Technology/design problems (pop-ups)
> History (family happenings)
> Music (songs and music to amuse, music-making)
> Art (cartoons, model-making, funny faces)
> Physical education (gymnastic skills)
> RE, moral education (teasing etc.)
> and drama (clown routines, showing emotion, for example happiness, sadness).

The only aim not met is to work on geography. This could be put into the timetable as a separate subject. However, the timetable does begin to look overloaded, so it may be better to ensure that geography predominates in the next topic tackled by these children.

In addition to the intended coverage listed in the aims, the topic work also provides opportunities for some learning in mathematics (times of TV programmes and two- and three-dimensional shapes). This work could be structured to meet the requirements of, for example, the programme of study elements, interpreting numbers and sorting two- and three-dimensional shapes; such work would be pitched at level 3, attainment targets 3, 8 and 10.

Figure 4.1 Topic Web T1

Focus: Two groups of children in a Y3 class (1st year juniors), about 10–12 children

Topic title: WHAT'S SO FUNNY?

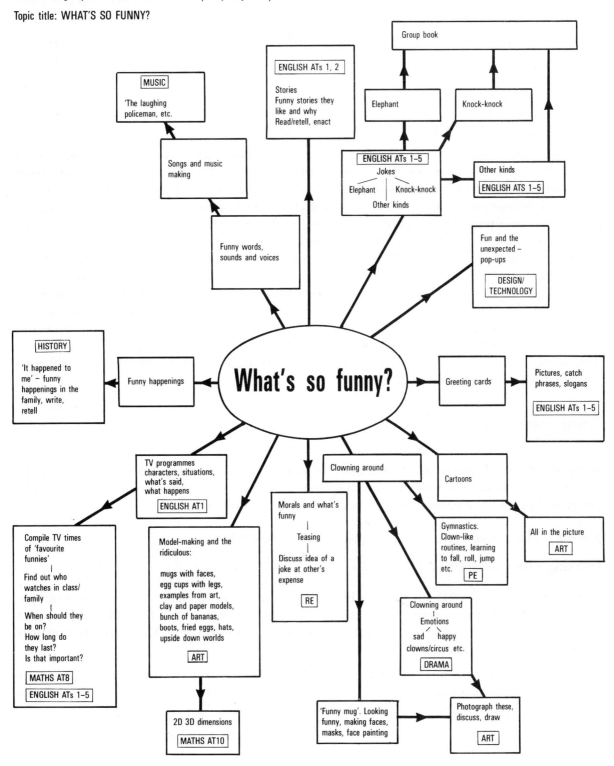

Teaching time and group topic work   In order to run a topic for some children in the class while others are pursuing a regular timetable, strategies have to be worked out for the teacher to spend more time and attention on the topic groups for part of the day. This can be made easier by:

- ▶ labelling everything needed and training the children to fetch their own resources

- ▶ giving the rest of the class revision and rehearsal work rather than new learning

- ▶ being didactic with the rest of the class.

Because the teacher is required to monitor the work of the rest of the class, while working with the topic groups, a teacher timetable is a useful addition to the usual pupil timetable. A sample week is presented in Figure 4.2. It shows the teacher when he or she should have time with the topic groups while carrying out a supervisory role with the other children. In order to show at a glance how the teacher's time is allocated, the timetable also shows what area of learning the children are working on. It may be topic work or subject work. It can be seen that the topic work groups are engaged in a range of activities in the topic sessions, and are doing subject work for the rest of the time. The children not involved in the topic are doing work in the core and foundation subjects, and a sense of curriculum balance is being achieved. The complex form of timetable should be seen as a teacher timetable overlaid on a pupil timetable, and has been set out in this way so that readers do not have to cross reference from one page to another. The overlaying of one timetable on another is simply for the purposes of this book. In practice it is probably easier to write a timetable for the teacher to be put alongside a timetable for the children. The two timetables are useful additions to teaching plans.

Topic plan T2

Age of children and groupings   A Y6 class (top juniors) operating at levels 2–6. For this topic, the class has been divided into two groups, the more able and the less able. Some activities will be attempted by all the children, but not necessarily at the same time.

Timing   Mid-autumn term, to finish just before 5 November.

Working title   'Explosions'.

Aims   In English: to work on some of the elements in the programme of study, for example, giving and responding to instructions, discussing explanations, writing for different purposes, writing descriptions, reading to learn, using books to locate information. These activities relate to the English attainment targets 1–5.

In science: to work on some of the elements in the programme of study; for example, raising and answering questions, safety and care, experience of forces. The children will be working on attainment targets 1, 9 and 10.

There should also be an opportunity to work in the following foundation subjects: geography, history, music, art, and PE.

Figure 4.2 A timetable to allow topic work for two groups of children in a Y3 class, while the rest of the class pursue their regular work

		SESSION 1 a.m.	SESSION 2 a.m.	SESSION 3 p.m.
MON	TEACHER	Chair whole class discussion	Help topic groups redraft stories. Give minimal help with computation to rest of class	Teach gymnastics to whole class / Chair whole class discussion. Show weather map. Establish knowledge. Give key words. *Science*
	TOPIC GROUPS	*Topic/English* Discuss weekend news/funny events as whole class	*Topic* Redraft story. Best copy for class book. Illustrate.	*Topic/PE* Floorwork on rolls/falls/funny walks. Apparatus work to develop. / Discuss weather. Study weather to map. Learn key words.
	REST OF CLASS	*English* Write news/funny story in English books	*Mathematics* Mathematics computation practice	*English* Listen to story. Respond to teacher requests. / Collate weather display
TUES	TEACHER	Direct children not working on topic to read quietly / Work with topic groups to start compiling joke book. / Teach and monitor hand-writing with rest of class. Group poetry reading.	Talk about pencil technique work to whole class. Show, for example, shading, cross-hatching, light and dark. Supervise class artwork.	Chair weather discussion. Talk about 'reporting'. Read weather report. Supervise classwork.
	TOPIC GROUPS	*Topic* Compile joke book using class and own resources. Work co-operatively as groups.	*Topic* Produce illustrations for joke books using pencil techniques	*Science* Subject theme: weather. Talk about kinds of weather, current weather conditions. All children write a weather report/draw a weather picture/devise a weather sign. Make it. Add to display.
	REST OF CLASS	*English* Quiet reading / Handwriting / Group poetry reading	*Art* Using a pencil, experiment with light and shade – drawing shadows in or from the classroom	Watch and comment on weather sign collation.

Weekend / Session 1 a.m. teacher note (MON): Supervise/help all children with vocabulary, spelling and writing

MON, TOPIC GROUPS Session 1: Write funny story – 'It happened to me', in draft

MON, Session 3 p.m. TEACHER: Read story. Ask children to bring in jokes, comics and weather maps. *English*

43

Figure 4.2 (continued)

	SESSION 1 a.m.	SESSION 2 a.m.	SESSION 3 p.m.
TEACHER	Direct topic groups to do computation practice / Work on new mathematics concepts with rest of class, teaching and helping with recording	With whole class, prepare for TV programmes; watch it and follow up with discussion / Direct rest of class to record / Show face pictures to topic groups. Discuss. Help with mask design.	Work with topic groups; monitor co-operation etc. Take photographs. Clean up. / Hear reading; individual reading development sessions
TOPIC GROUPS	*Mathematics* — Mathematics computation practice	*History* — Lead in, watch and follow up TV history programme. Compile key word list and learn where to get resources. / *Topic* — Look at faces, elements of a face – why funny? Design a mask.	*Topic* — Face paint in pairs. Photograph session. Clean up. / *English* — Quiet reading. Reading follow-up to history programme. Quiet reading for pleasure.
REST OF CLASS	Work on new concepts in mathematics. Do some recording.	*History* — Record response to TV programme. Use key words and resources.	*History* — Finish, recording about TV programme. Illustrate.

W E D N E S D A Y

Figure 4.2 (continued)

		SESSION 1 a.m.	SESSION 2 a.m.	SESSION 3 p.m.
THURSDAY	TEACHER	Direct rest of class to read quietly · Show topic groups how to retrieve programmes and their times from *Radio/TV Times* · With rest of class, work on new maths concepts · Help topic groups with further TV times recording	Set rest of class going on weather design problem · Work on new mathematics concepts with topic groups · Discuss design problems, assumptions, next steps with rest of class *[Mathematics]*	Set rest of class to record weather activities · Help topic groups with questionnaire compilation. Assist individual children across whole class. · Read story *[English]*
	TOPIC GROUPS	*[Topic]* Study old *TV Times* and *Radio Times* and list funny programmes as group or in two groups · Further recording – times of programme, programme duration, who in their family watches	*[Topic]* Quiet group discussion about TV · *[Mathematics]* Work on new mathematics concepts. Do some recording.	*[Topic]* Compile questionnaire about favourite funny TV programmes. In pairs interview two people in the school and record replies. · *[English]* Story
	REST OF CLASS	*[English]* Quiet reading · *[Mathematics]* Work on new concepts · *[Science]* Weather quizsheet on common symbols	*[Science]* Design something to measure rainfall, wind direction or wind speed. Draw. Discuss with teacher. Look at instruments in current use. Decide location for school weather station.	*[Science]* Record activities re: weather monitoring
FRIDAY	TEACHER	*[Science]* Give topic groups weather quiz sheet · Introduce creative writing to rest of class · *[Topic]* Collate TV programme questionnaire. · Supervise monitor, supply vocabulary to whole class	Direct rest of class to do computation practice · *[Topic]* Discuss all TV programme work and ways of recording for topic books. Start to record. · Help topic groups to begin recording work on funny TV programmes	*[Topic]* Finishing recording on TV programme work. · Help topic groups with their recording. Discuss book choice, assist reading and review development with individual children from whole class.
	TOPIC GROUPS	*[Mathematics]* Work on new concepts		*[English]* Reading for topic – funny stories. Read for pleasure.
	REST OF CLASS	*[English]* Creative writing task, using Tuesday's poetry or 'weather' as a stimulus	*[Mathematics]* Mathematics computation practice	*[English]* Reading and book review discussion. Read for pleasure.

Figure 4.3   Topic web T2
Focus: A Y6 (top junior) class

Topic title: EXPLOSIONS

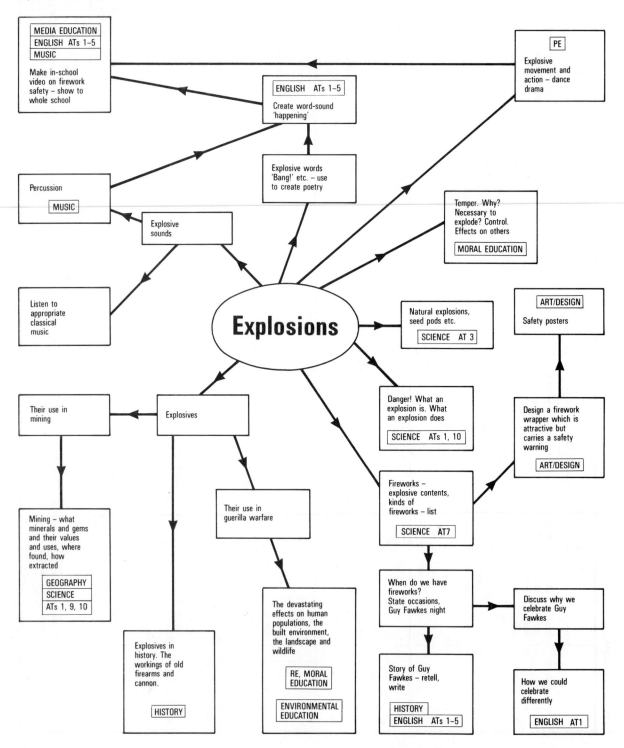

Figure 4.4 A list of activities for a class of top juniors (Y6) working at levels 2–6 when engaged on a topic entitled: 'Explosions'. Activities have been listed for more and less able children, separately.

ACTIVITIES FOR THE MORE ABLE CHILDREN	ACTIVITIES FOR THE LESS ABLE CHILDREN
ENGLISH English ATs 1–5	**ENGLISH** English ATs 1–5
Explosive words list – discuss – read and create poetry. Create class display of poetry as reading resource. Write script for school firework safety video.	Explosive words list – discuss – draw – colour – annotate and display. For example:
SCIENCE/GEOGRAPHY Science ATs 1, 3, 7, 9, 10	**SCIENCE/GEOGRAPHY** Science ATs 1, 7, 9, 10
Danger – fireworks – how they work. Mining – list what is mined and how. Details of extraction process. Discuss where in world mining happens. Use globe and world maps. draw and identify mineral distribution world-wide on duplicated maps. Natural explosions. Research seed pods that burst etc. Write up for class resource book.	Danger – fireworks – how they work. Mining – list some things mined and, briefly, how. Choose two or three minerals to focus on, for example, coal, gold. Discuss where these are mined. Colour mineral–rich areas of the continents.
HISTORY	**HISTORY**
Old firearms and cannon (models or museum loan). Discuss workings. Draw and label. Answer written questions about them using resource books and retrieving information. Guy Fawkes. Rewrite the story of the events leading up to and during the Gunpowder Plot saga, after appropriate research and discussion.	Old firearms and cannon (models or museum loan). Discuss workings. Draw and label. Guy Fawkes. Retell orally the story of the events. Draw captioned pictures to record the story.
PE/DRAMA/DANCE	**PE/DRAMA/DANCE**
Floorwork. Explosive movement, stageshow routines, disco dancing. Enact script for firework safety video.	Floorwork. Explosive movement, stage show routines, disco dancing. Enact non-speaking parts for firework safety video.
MUSIC (Possibly science AT14)	**MUSIC** (Possibly science AT14)
Explosive music – listening, appreciation, for example Carl Orff, Handel. Percussion sounds, their orchestration.	Explosive music – listening, appreciation, for example Carl Orff, Handel. Percussion sounds, their orchestration. Produce sound track for firework safety video.
ART (Possibly mathematics ATs 8, 11)	**ART** (Possibly mathematics ATs 8, 11)
Explosive art and design. Look at work of artists like Klee and Warhol. Design firework wrappers, safety posters and safety warnings.	Explosive art and design. Look at work of artists like Klee and Warhol. Design firework wrappers, safety posters and safety warnings.
RE, MORAL AND ENVIRONMENTAL EDUCATION (Possibly science AT5)	**RE, MORAL AND ENVIRONMENTAL EDUCATION** (Possibly science AT5)
Celebrations – why and how. Firework danger. Guerilla warfare – discuss effects on human populations, built environment, landscapes and wildlife. Temper. Discuss ways to diffuse and control.	Celebrations – why we celebrate Guy Fawkes. Firework danger. Guerilla warfare – discuss effects in brief. Temper – discuss ways to diffuse and control.

FINALE
With teacher as cameraman, rehearse and record firework safety video – script produced by more able, sound effects by less able, posters and captions by all the children, and all the class taking part. Show it to the school. Add to school resources.

Topic title   The topic title is 'Explosions', and this has provided the stimulus word for the heart of the topic web set out in Figure 4.3.

Timetable planning   When planning the timetable, two lists of activities were drawn up, one for the more able children and the other for the less able. These are set out in Figure 4.4, along with the appropriate attainment targets. This topic work demonstrates that all the children can be allowed access to the whole curriculum be they more or less able.

Topic plan T3

Age of children and groupings   An R, Y1, Y2 class (family-grouped infants) operating at levels 1–3, and placed in interest/friendship groups for this work.

Timing   It could be done at any time during the school year.

Working title   'Homes'.

Figure 4.5   Topic web T3a
Focus: A R, Y1, Y2 (Family-grouped infant) class

Topic title: YOUR HOUSE, MY HOUSE

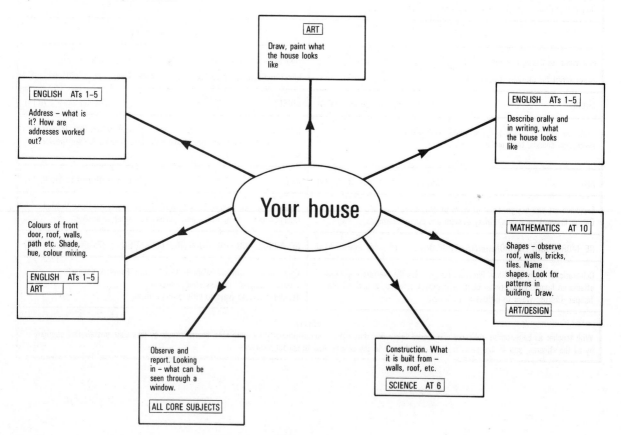

48

Aims   In English: to work on some of the elements in the programme of study, for example, responding to complex instructions and questions, talking about things done, discussing work, recording observations and working with other children. These activities relate to the English attainment targets 1–5.

In mathematics: to work on some of the elements in the programme of study, for example, counting, reading and writing numbers, sorting, classifying, building and drawing shapes, comparing dimensions, recording by drawing, the beginnings of lists and tables. Work will relate to mathematics attainment targets 2, 5, 8, 9, 10 and 13.

In science: to work on some of the elements in the programme of study, for example, sorting, grouping, describing similarities and differences, systematic recording. Work will relate to science attainment targets 1 and 6.

Final topic title   The final topic title is 'Your house: my house'. The children have already done some topic work on animal homes, looking at the shapes and sizes, and methods and materials used in construction. The intention is to look at human homes in similar terms and compare them with one another.

Topic web   Most activities will be the same for 'Your house' and 'My house', so the topic is to be split into two webs. The topic webs, T3a and T3b, have been drawn up in Figures 4.5 and 4.6. The plan is to implement web T3a first.

Repetition of activities in this topic   The children in a family-grouped infant class have a wide range of abilities, and some children are more mature than others and settle into the school routines more confidently. If the children have the chance to try a range of activities concerning one house, and then do some similar activities when working on their own home, this will promote:

- ▶ consolidation for slow learners
- ▶ further development and sophistication for abler children
- ▶ increasing confidence to tackle tasks
- ▶ the development of memory skills.

Final planning details   The initial aims have been met, and work in art is added. Assessment and evaluation strategies can now be worked out and a timetable of activities compiled. The children will either be taken on a trip to look at a really big house, or will be taken on a walk round a house near school. In some schools it may be possible for them to compare a friend's house with their own. 'Your house' could then be the big house, the school neighbour's house, or a friend's house. If the children work on 'Your house' first, followed by the work on 'My house', comparisons will be possible. The children should be able to point them out by laying their work pieces side by side.

Figure 4.6 Topic web T3b
Focus: A R, Y1, Y2 (Family-grouped infant) class

Topic title: YOUR HOUSE, MY HOUSE

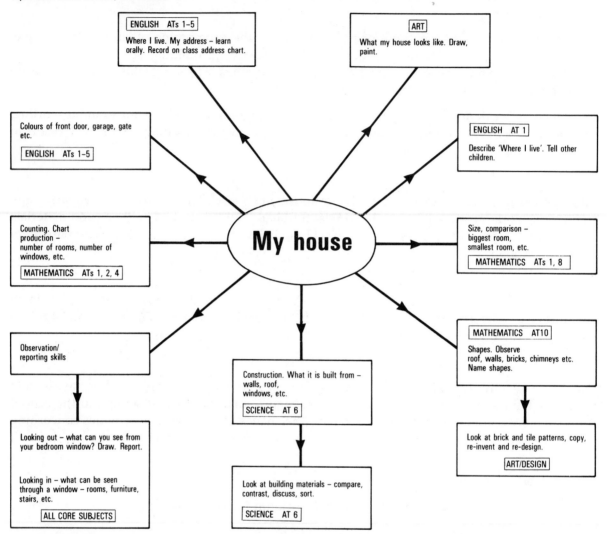

ENGLISH ATs 1–5

Where I live. My address – learn orally. Record on class address chart.

ART

What my house looks like. Draw, paint.

Colours of front door, garage, gate etc.

ENGLISH ATs 1–5

ENGLISH AT 1

Describe 'Where I live'. Tell other children.

Counting. Chart production – number of rooms, number of windows, etc.

MATHEMATICS ATs 1, 2, 4

My house

Size, comparison – biggest room, smallest room, etc.

MATHEMATICS ATs 1, 8

Observation/ reporting skills

MATHEMATICS AT10

Shapes. Observe roof, walls, bricks, chimneys etc. Name shapes.

Construction. What it is built from – walls, roof, windows, etc.

SCIENCE AT 6

Looking out – what can you see from your bedroom window? Draw. Report.

Looking in – what can be seen through a window – rooms, furniture, stairs, etc.

ALL CORE SUBJECTS

Look at building materials – compare, contrast, discuss, sort.

SCIENCE AT 6

Look at brick and tile patterns, copy, re-invent and re-design.

ART/DESIGN

Topic plan T4

Age of children and groupings A Y3, Y4 class (lower juniors, family grouped) working levels 2–4.

Timing The work should be done in the spring or summer terms, as it involves planting and growing seeds.

Working title 'Under glass'.

Aims The work is intended to meet the following requirements of the programmes of study:

Figure 4.7   Topic web T4
Focus: A Y3, Y4 (Family-grouped lower junior) class, working at levels 2–4

Topic title: UNDER GLASS

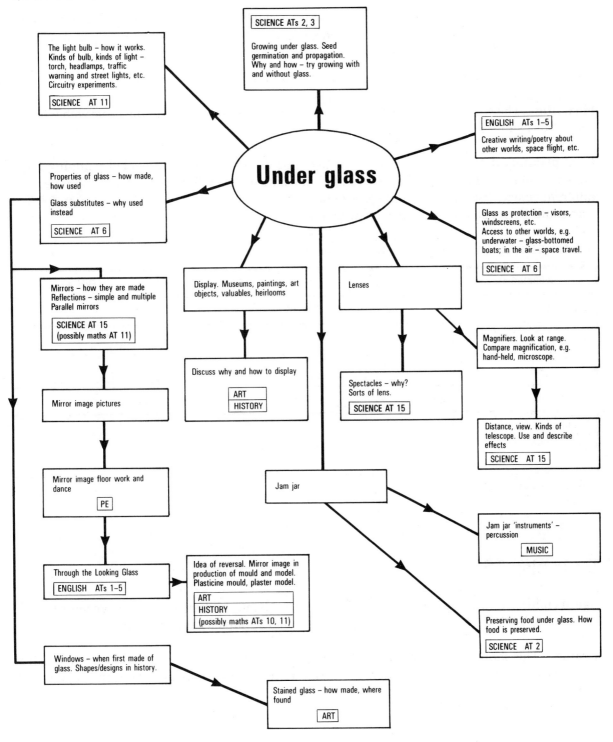

In English: for example, giving and responding to instructions, collecting data, reading non-fiction and poetry, locating information, writing poetry and prose. This work will meet the English attainment targets 1–5.

In science: for example, developing investigative skills, environmental conditions and their effects on plants, circuit construction, investigation of light passing through transparent objects, mirror images. This work will meet science attainment targets 1, 2, 11 and 15.

There should also be an opportunity to do work in art, history, music and PE.

Final title   The working title seems appropriate and will fit the centre of the topic web which is set out in Figure 4.7.

Final planning details   The web does fit the aims as set out above. Detailed planning must, however, allow all the children to be extended, at whatever level they are working. In timetabling, different activity lists can be compiled for children working at each of the levels 2, 3 and 4. The lists could be set side by side as in Figure 4.8.

Figure 4.8   Topic timetable layout, for children working at different levels

WORKING AT:	LEVEL 2	LEVEL 3	LEVEL 4
SCIENCE	ATs	ATs	ATs
Activities			
MATHEMATICS	ATs	ATs	ATs
Activities			

And so on for all subjects covered in the topic

Topic plan T5

Age of children and groupings   A primary school, with the children arranged in year groups (R, Y1, Y2, Y3, Y4, Y5, Y6), and then arranged in smaller groups as appropriate.

Timing   This should be worked through during the second half of the autumn term, to finish at Christmas. The topic does not cut across the traditions of Christmas, and the resulting displays will be impressive.

Working title   'Decoration'.

Figure 4.9 Topic web T5
Focus: A primary school (R, Y1, Y2, Y3, Y4, Y5, Y6)

Topic title: DECORATION

Note: Subject titles have been omitted in this topic web, for the strands are not always subject-specific and need further refinement, to justify a subject label. For example 'make-up' involves aspects of art, history, geography, science and design.

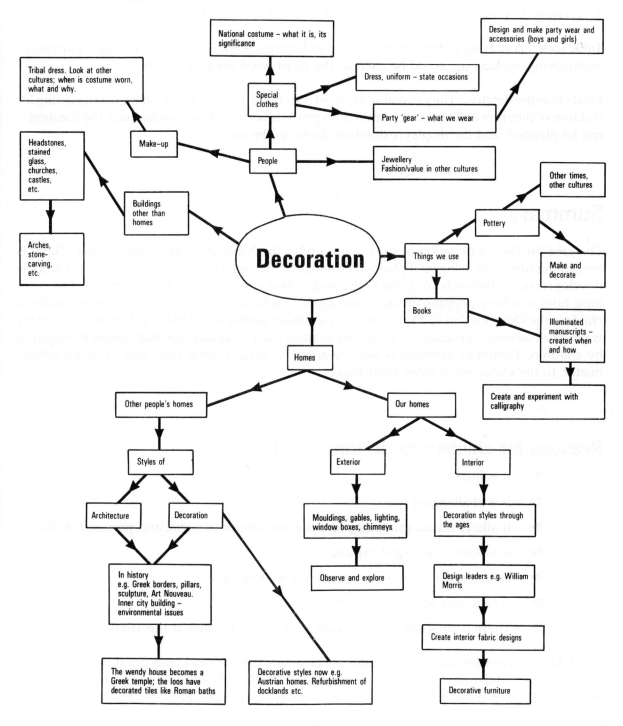

Aims   The topic work is art-based with associated history and geography investigations and enquiries. Through the topic all the children will work on elements of the English programmes of study leading to attainment targets 1–5.

Final topic title   A final title may need to be created for each class or section or department. 'Decoration' is very broad, and like other catch-all titles, needs further refinement.

Topic web   A starting web has been created in Figure 4.9. Each strand, for example partywear, bookmaking, making up, could be used as the heart word for a new web.

Final planning details   The general aims, as set out above, are met, but need more structuring for children of different abilities. Once evaluation procedures have been worked out, the timetables can be planned, and the display/exhibition dates can be set.

Summary

The case for the continuation of topic work under the National Curriculum is clear. There is everything to gain in using well planned cross-curricular approaches providing that the work is developed in a whole-school context. The major danger in topic work is repetition. There are topic titles that keep popping up again and again. Teachers have argued that it doesn't matter if children do 'Ourselves' in R, Y1, Y3 etc. for the subject matter is tackled in increasingly complex ways. The National Curriculum actually delineates a body of knowledge that should be acquired by children. Thorough planning is now required to avoid undue repetition of some subject matter, to the exclusion of other knowledge.

Repetition of topic.

Reasons for children to do topic work

▶   It is interesting.

▶   It is challenging.

▶   It allows mixed groupings and the emergence of social and personal skills.

▶   It is open-ended and exploratory.

▶   It breaks the routine of a conventional timetable.

▶   It facilitates home-school links.

▶   There is progress in several areas of learning, often at the same time.

For children there seems only one possible shortcoming to topic work, and that is that every child needs to form a learning framework, in order to make links between different subjects. Some children will need more help than others in making connections between ideas.

Reasons for teacher to do topic work

▶ It is lively and stimulating for the teacher to plan and execute.

▶ The children are more motivated (resulting, perhaps, in fewer discipline problems).

▶ Assessment on several fronts is possible (often at the same time).

The implementation of the National Curriculum does mean that whether teaching is done through subjects or topics, the planning will be complex.

C

MANAGING THE NATIONAL CURRICULUM

This section is concerned with central issues to do with the organisation and management of the National Curriculum in the school as a whole and in the classroom. It aims to give support in:

▶ offering appropriate learning opportunities

▶ increasing the amount of children's time on task

▶ efficient delivery of the curriculum

▶ collaborative activity and team work.

Introduction

An important precept underpinning the National Curriculum is that teachers are effective managers of learning. This is not a novel view but the expectations it brings must now be explored at a level of detail that may be new to many teachers. The National Curriculum Council is clearly concerned to be seen as supportive of good primary practice. Whilst definitions of good practice are difficult to agree upon, there are clearly some common themes which run through all discussions. Overall planning, teamwork, commitment and planned resourcing are central to good practice and good management.

Planning and aims

It is a mistake to always plan whole-school development on the basis of our knowledge of certain children. Planning for the future must be about the predicted needs of all children. This may seem heretical as we are all carers who put our major effort into the development of relationships and learning opportunities for the children in our school at the present time. But the problem about planning around today's issues is that they are built into tomorrow in a way which makes purposeful development very difficult. It is important, therefore, to periodically suspend our involvement in the hurly-burly of our daily work and to ask ourselves a set of questions of the 'what if?' kind.

This does not mean we should be always starting with a blank sheet of paper and musing on our Utopian school, but we should do it sometimes. It helps us clarify issues to do with developmental changes, in-service needs and administrative systems; enabling us, in short, to start to see the wood and not just the trees. One of the advantages that the National Curriculum brings is that your curriculum objectives will be easier to validate. In turn this will lead to a clearer consensus on aims. This does not mean that every school's aims will or should be the same; local initiatives and priorities must be taken into account.

The importance of people management

Because education is a people business and people, whether oneself, child or colleague, are constantly changing their aspirations and so their needs, the 'teacher as manager' is an active role which involves planning, initiating, monitoring and implementing change. If this begins to look like 'teacher as evaluator' it is not accidental. The two skills, management and evaluation, are heavily interdependent. They are, indeed, the watchwords for the nineties.

All of you are leaders for part of the time, certainly in your own classrooms. Leadership is seen as a positive attribute when used to describe individuals but it is important not to confuse leadership with being a 'boss'. Leaders bring out qualities, they do not suppress them in the interests of preserving their own status or dignity.

A major strength of primary schools is their capacity to involve a comparatively small group of teachers in a common enterprise which is all about whole experiences. But therein also lies a weakness. Schools can become too inward-looking and over-dependent on in-house appraisal of standards and performance. It is essential that staff work as a team whilst incorporating outside views and new or alternative ideas.

Management demands of the National Curriculum

The National Curriculum offers us many possibilities and problems. How these will be grasped and dealt with will not only depend on our personal qualities but also on our ability to organise and manage appropriate learning opportunities for our classes. This sort of management need is not in fact new or exclusive to National Curriculum initiatives; schools and classrooms have always been managed. What we now need to do is to concentrate our management ideas on the best ways we can change our institutions into strong ones with a faster dynamic in which children can flourish within the climate set up by the National Curriculum.

This section concentrates on people as the major influence in managing such an environment. People will need support in terms of a coherent resourcing policy, and they will need to understand the demands of innovation and change. Such things are discussed in the following pages but we must not forget that at the heart of the system is the quality of relationship and communication which exists between learner and teacher. Sensitive and forward-looking management of the people in the system is the engine which will drive not just the National Curriculum but a whole and wholesome curriculum.

CHAPTER 5

MANAGING PEOPLE

Education is about developing the potential of children (and teachers), but this involves more than focusing exclusively on individual children's experiences. Some teachers, however, seem to start and finish there. They say things like, 'I'm here for the children, they are all that matters.' Of course in one sense this is so, but to spend all our time focusing on the appropriate work tasks for Lewis and Jane in J3 means that we make no attempt to harness all the aspects of the school to best effect. As contemporary HMI reports stress, in schools where good practice occurs, detailed planning is always a factor and it engages the whole staff.

The key problem is how to plan, develop and deliver, in a flexible way, the whole school curriculum, looking beyond the perimeter of the immediate situation. For example, even though the whole curriculum can only include, say, country dancing, if there is a member of staff able to teach it, this does not mean that planning for all developments should be framed by current staffing. Staff changes can transform a school, and such change can be disturbingly rapid if there is no set of aims and objectives to which new staff are introduced. Therefore school development plans should engage closely with staffing, staff development and the wider community.

With the whole curriculum, present and future, in mind, these are the issues to address:

> Teamwork and staff deployment
> Staff development and INSET
> Leadership
> Time management
> Communication, both internally and with parents, governors and other schools
> Groupings of children within and across classes.

We will look at each of these in turn.

Teamwork and staff deployment

A whole-school plan for curriculum delivery will set out what is to be considered in allocating teaching roles to individual staff members. The curriculum may be broken down in many ways. Some of these possible ways have been mentioned in Chapter 3. They may result in, for example, individual teachers being labelled as: areas of knowledge specialist; subject specialist; level specialist; and strategic specialist (assessment, resources, etc.).

Building teams

In building teams it is necessary to consider the balance of expertise in all dimensions of the whole curriculum and try to ensure that these are represented. Recent planning and teacher training have focused on the use of curriculum leaders and consultants in predominantly subject areas, but it is also important to give status to other kinds of expertise. It is not the case that teachers stay with their subject; they may well have developed other interests in addition to those they studied when training. Such flexibility is one of the major strengths of the primary teacher and will support the development of new plans and strategies.

Team meetings

Due to the size of schools, and to the complex nature of primary schooling, it is essential that all staff assume responsibility for more than one area of experience. If age-related groupings continue, then the first assigned role for each teacher will be to a class. But beyond that it is possible, through negotiation, recruitment and staff development, to enhance class teacher profiles in a way which allows them to operate through the school. This means that there must be opportunities for regular team meetings. Teams can exist which are sub-sets of the staff. National Curriculum work will necessitate liaison between teachers in a way that may not have happened before.

Staff development and INSET

Curriculum development and staff development

Curriculum development is essentially about staff development. The introduction of National Curriculum is not development, it is the provision of a content framework. The improvement of the curriculum will embrace teaching and learning as well as content, and it can only take place through school-based activities, which will hinge on the insights of teachers, and, crucially, on their own intellectual growth.

To manage the establishment of an appropriate curriculum which meets both the children's needs and the national requirements, schools will evaluate their organisational and delivery systems, their teaching strengths and, through staff evaluation and appraisal, identify areas of deficit or potential weakness. These can be remediated through in-service training.

What is staff development?

Staff development is complex. It has to do with meeting school needs, career intentions and personal preferences. It is important to distinguish between those activities which support the school's needs and those which refresh and extend individual teachers in a broader sense. The two need not be incompatible, but the first is for the here and now and the second is for the future and the wider education system.

Staff development involves a consideration of:

- ▶ individual teacher career paths
- ▶ resourcing the curriculum, through the development of expertise in particular teachers
- ▶ whole-staff learning ventures.

Individual career development

A common problem is that of a teacher whose career is not progressing as he or she might wish. They are not being given the learning opportunities which they need to parallel the children's learning. We have set out an example using strategies for looking at this problem. Our approach is similar to tactics we use in evaluation (see Chapter 8) and this is not accidental. Evaluation is essential to good management.

Problem   Why is my career not developing as I had hoped? I am still a main scale incentive A teacher and feel I have had little chance for self-development.

Information collection   The teacher charts his/her career to date, and writes down all the plus factors, things learned, and responsibilities held in his/her present job and jobs done in the past.

Reflection   The teacher lists points of change needed to achieve career development, including change of location, school, age group, department, level of job. He/she makes a list of personal strengths: 'What am I good at?' 'What do I like doing?'; and weaknesses: 'Where do I need to be more controlled?' 'What do I need to learn more about?' 'In what curriculum areas can I do more?'

Action   The teacher asks for a development discussion with the headteacher, where he/she explains some of his/her thinking and suggests proposed strategies. He/she listens to the advice offered, and plans a course of action, for example, 'I need practice in speaking to an adult audience so I shall volunteer to speak at the next PTA meeting'; 'In order to get the job I should like I need to know more about science – I shall go on a course'.

Commentary

It is part of the headteacher's role to help, not only with the intellectual development of the children in the school, but also with that of the staff. Ask him or her if you may consult on a regular basis to discuss your development. The introduction of staff appraisal should support this type of consultation, providing it is about development and not just performance. Professional development needs planning and you should look beyond the short course towards developing a coherent sequence of activities. If you do plan your development it strengthens your arguments when negotiating for in-service opportunities.

Developing subject expertise

The introduction of the National Curriculum means that the whole staff of each school will need to work out who has expertise (which may be hidden) in what curriculum areas. Schools cannot afford to pass up any opportunity to use the considerable talents and potential of the staff. To exploit them fully may require an effort of exploration and investment in training, but the benefits to teachers and children will justify both.

Teachers as learners   Strangely enough, some teachers are reluctant to take on new learning. Maybe this is because of the notion that it is easier to do things the way they have always done them; also, they do not want to take on a challenge for fear that success may not come quickly or easily to them – in other words they are afraid of failing. There is, however, another important reason why some teachers have to be pressed into going on courses, which is that the provision of good learning opportunities for teachers is very patchy. Some in-service courses are a total waste of time, money, interest and enthusiasm. They do not provide access to knowledge; they do not engage teachers appropriately; and they do not match the teachers' learning needs.

On the other hand there are teachers who feel compelled to attend courses they dislike, in the hope of appeasing their colleagues or headteacher. This never has been a good management gambit. All teachers know about recalcitrant learners.

Perhaps now we can do something about these quite valid reasons for teachers being reluctant to take up learning opportunities. In fact, we believe that few people will be able to go on, under the National Curriculum, doing things in exactly the same way as they have always done. We need help, support and encouragement, as adult learners, just as we did when we were children, and not least as we tackle the task of learning the content of the National Curriculum and the management skills it requires. To ensure that a course does meet your needs, you can:

> ▶   find out what it is about before you say you will go

> ▶   find out for whom it is intended, so that you will not end up taking a place on a course which may be over-subscribed, only to find its content too simple or too sophisticated

> ▶   ensure, before it starts, that you can contribute to its evaluation, so that what is best about it can be repeated.

Commentary

> ▶ Plan aims and objectives for yourself each term.
>
> ▶ Make sure courses you attend fit your own learning programme as well as that for the department and school.
>
> ▶ Do not block avenues to learning, simply because you:
> 'have never done it'
> 'know nothing about it'
> 'cannot do it anyway'.
>
> Remember, if you cannot do it, it may be because you yourself were badly taught. You are now being given another chance to learn, and thereby to better help children in your care. Then they can avoid the position of having to say, 'I cannot do it.'

In the following example a teacher is required to develop her subject expertise.

Problem The teacher has been given responsibility for the science curriculum planning in school. Though she has A-level biology, she has done no science since then and she lacks confidence.

Reflection She can find out the following:

▶ What is the National Curriculum for science?

▶ Are there other members of staff with scientific expertise, whom she can consult?

▶ Are there staff in other neighbouring schools who will help?

▶ What books are available in school, both in the children's library and staff library?

▶ What resources are available in school and in neighbouring schools?

▶ What is for sale in catalogues? What money is the school likely to be able to spend on science resources?

▶ What additional books and other resources do the children need?

▶ What additional books and other resources do the staff need?

Action   The teacher can now compile an action list starting with resources, to identify people who can be consulted, and things needed; what they are and where they can be found. She can talk to the science adviser about resourcing. She can also go on a course or, if no suitable course can be found, ask for one for the next closure.

Commentary

Taking on a curriculum leadership role means taking initiatives. Decision-making is crucial to the role, but this does not mean there is no consultation. If you are going to extend a subject area, you need to share ideas, both inside and outside school. This means that as you gain confidence and knowledge, you must find ways of engaging colleagues and not instructing them. If you instruct you will find yourself having to do all the preparation, planning and resourcing for everyone. That is not leadership. It is servitude!

Whole-staff development

Development of the staff as a whole may be necessary where there are areas of knowledge in which no one on the staff professes to have any expertise. Small schools sometimes face this dilemma. It affects some larger schools in 'new' curriculum areas like IT and technology. In the following example, we suggest management strategies to deal with the problem of using computers.

Problem   The introduction of computers into school has not changed the collective staff suspicion of things technological. Having the computer wheeled into the classroom for an hour a week does not mean it has been incorporated into the curriculum. The children, who have never known a world without TV, cashpoints and computer-operated supermarket checkouts, do not share staff unease. The IT demands of the National Curriculum are going to make it imperative, not only that staff overcome their suspicion, but that they also achieve computer literacy.

Information collection   The whole staff meet to discuss computers, where the head, a visiting speaker or the appropriate staff member explains the trends in IT, and the kinds of skills teachers and children will require. The following issues can be discussed:

> Problems in present knowledge
> Access to hardware
> Access to software
> Resourcing, (for example, how many manuals are there?)
> Timetabling for teacher
> Timetabling for children
> Supervision
> Setting up
> How to use
> Staff access out of school time.

Reflection As a group the staff compile a checklist, based on the results of discussion, to highlight the problems.

Action As a staff, act on the problem checklist, an item at a time. Here are some possibilities for action:

▶ Undertake a computer resource evaluation. List hardware, find out what it does, read manuals, try software, search catalogues to identify possible additions to resources.

▶ Set up school in-house training. This could be a rolling process: one member of staff teaches start-up, load etc., then staff work in pairs to master the software.

▶ Build computer literacy into the internal school curriculum; then it cannot be overlooked.

▶ School closure with computer literacy as its focus.

▶ Search out computer competence in the children and invite them to teach teacher.

Commentary

To attack the issue in the way we have suggested does mean that staff will have to expose their concerns about new technologies. The best approach may be to consider the learning opportunities we want to offer the children and how these may be resourced. It is important to keep in mind that books were once new technologies. The use of computers extends teachers' and children's abilities to collect and organise information and their thinking.

Leadership

The headteacher as leader

The head imposes his or her own management style on a school. Under the National Curriculum this will, no doubt, continue to be the case. The aspects of managing in school which most commonly come into the head's job description are public relations, finance and staffing. Since the head is often the only staff member not in class all day, the contact with the outside world must be maintained through him or her. The head may be stuck with the administration of finance, too, unless schools hire the services of a bursar or accountant. The staffing problem is increasingly one to solve in consultation with the whole staff.

Curriculum leadership

Subject specialists and others in posts of responsibility should be prepared to carry through their management responsibilities without constant reference to the head. Here is an example of how such a management dilemma can be carried through without the head's intervention.

Problem   Dissemination. The English consultant in the school has a diploma in language work with young children, and a language background, but needs to share her expertise more with colleagues, in the light of the National Curriculum requirements.

Information collection   She can talk individually to colleagues about what they see as problems for them in English teaching, and any special issues the National Curriculum raises. Out of these conversations she can produce a set of statements which staff could be invited to respond to in terms of their relative importance.

Reflection   The issue is how to address problems raised by colleagues and items which she, herself, sees as important, for example:

> Planning
> Resourcing
> Stimuli for writing
> Choice of material
> Reading progress
> Marking
> Continuous assessment.

Action   If the same problem is mentioned or ranked as being high in importance by a number of staff, she should consider: a lunchtime workshop; a closure; or a working group.

If it is a problem for a single teacher, she could arrange to spend time with that teacher, in and out of class, until the problem is overcome. With the help of other staff, that teacher could be released to observe while the consultant is teaching the children in class.

Commentary

The sort of professional activity just described is taking place all of the time. However, in many schools the traditions of headship and the niceness of teachers has prevented them taking up fully these management responsibilities. It is not uncommon for teachers to describe themselves as being on the shop floor. If we press this metaphor then it is really the children who are actually on the shop floor. All teachers are management! The National Curriculum lays bare the necessity to be practising managers. Avoiding unnecessary delegation to the head involves professional trust between headteachers and their teams.

Time management

Preventing time loss: planning and timetabling

There is so much to do that teachers will have to manage both their own and children's time, so as to maximise that spent on teaching and learning.

Teacher time is learning time. Time lost in waiting for something to happen or a lunch hour that runs over cannot be recouped. How long does it take to line up, queue up, clear up and wait? Take away all that, and on some days there is not much time left. This time loss is most noticeable around fixed points in the school day and school term. Flexibility about playtime and lunch are, for many reasons including staffing, not possible. The same should not apply to assemblies, hall-time, library use, etc. When the whole class have to go somewhere else in the school, it makes sense to tie that activity to the end of a session, so that clearing up in class takes place before leaving, and the children then go off to play or lunch.

When you have a realistic timetable, which avoids class time loss, look at detailed planning and anticipate points at which time might be lost in lessons. For example, to save time you might:

- ▶ get everyone where they should be, before the lesson starts
- ▶ anticipate the resources needed and assemble them before the lesson (see Chapter 6)
- ▶ start on time – the most informal classrooms are managed flexibly by teachers who monitor time.

Preventing time loss: individual children

For a child, taking a message round the school may be independence building, but it is certainly disruptive, both to the learning of the child who carries the message and to those who receive the message. Tidying a cupboard may promote care for resources, but it wastes learning time. Those children who are asked to spend lesson time distributing new stock or emptying flower vases, or even sharpening pencils, are being abused. Teachers should not do these things in lesson time either.

Think before you ask a child to help another with learning. 'Peer group tutoring' has much to recommend it. But it is only appropriate when both children will gain from the exercise.

Preventing time loss: teacher

We all waste time. We do it in two ways. Firstly we do not examine how we actually spend time now. Secondly, we displace activities which are demanding, by doing other things. We say they are preparatory but they are actually time wasters.

There are two things you can do to work out where your time goes now:

1 Make a timetable for yourself (for example like that in Chapter 4).
2 Write down all the sorts of things you do, and over a week put a tick for every ten minutes you spend on them. If you list only teaching and learning tasks, the difference between total time ticked and the length of the school day will probably be time wasted.

Figure 5.1 is an example of such a time chart.

Figure 5.1   Time management: teacher time record

WEEK ENDING: Put a √ for every 10 minutes spent

DAY	TEACHING			PLANNING	RESOURCING	MARKING	COMMUNICATION		
	Class	Group	Individual				Head	Colleagues	Other
MONDAY									
TUESDAY									

To look now at displacement activities, at the heart of the difficulties of 'shortage of time' are workload and task management. There is no problem about actual time; there are 24 hours in a day! If you analyse why it is that some jobs never seem to get done you should consider whether they are: really important, lacking in team support, or incompatible with your organisation. If they are important tasks then it is necessary to focus on your organisational style and the nature of contributions made by or needed from colleagues.

Communication

With the emphasis on communication within the classroom, many schools are poor at communication to the outsider. Have you ever, as a visitor, spent time trying to find the main entrance or the secretary's office in another school? Schools tend to be inward-looking. This also affects communication between colleagues. Unless appropriate systems are formed, teachers can be isolated from many of the important influences and decisions. The areas for consideration in reviewing your communication network are how communication takes place between members of staff and with the community.

Communication within the school: formal and informal

The internal needs relate to what children need to know, what teachers need to know to inform children, and what teachers need to do to communicate with each other. There are formal and informal ways of passing on information in school. We shall look at these in turn. The formal ways include staff meetings, team meetings and internal record systems. Informal ways include the folder for circulation, the staffroom notice board, and of course chance conversations.

Staff meetings　These can be more efficiently managed by avoiding the dominance of the 'chair' held by the head. Where the head dominates some staff members never get involved in management issues beyond their class. Techniques which will be discussed in Chapter 6, such as small group discussions, are appropriate for staff meetings and resolve issues in ways compatible with the principles of teamwork.

Staff meetings need to:

> ▶ be regular
>
> ▶ involve everybody on the teaching staff and others (secretary, caretaker etc.) as appropriate
>
> ▶ have an agenda
>
> ▶ have a time limit – over-long meetings are not productive.

Team meetings　We cannot expect teamwork unless there are opportunities to talk, in a group, with colleagues. These meetings need to:

> ▶ occur more often than staff meetings
>
> ▶ involve everybody in the team (and others as necessary)
>
> ▶ have an agenda
>
> ▶ take place during directed time.

Internal record systems　A common format for reporting core (and later foundation) subject work, internal to school, is easy to produce and understandable to all. Such a format would promote effective communication. Chapter 10 on record keeping will help with this discussion. However, some across-curriculum work will probably happen too. This does pose different problems for the communication of topic content and achievement. The problems can be managed as suggested below.

Problem　Record keeping of topic work. Internal records of cross-curricular study have never been officially kept, though all class teachers have done topics. Class teachers' own records have not passed on with the child, and the standard internal report form has listed subjects. Topic work is now to be planned right across the school and the systematic recording of progress in topic work needs to be begun.

Information collection   Each teacher submits to a convenor the form of record she or he uses for topic work, including aims, objectives, webs, activities done, children's performance, progress markers.

Reflection   The convenor collates these and sets out preferred strategies, with noted additions required to fit the National Curriculum. For example: Is the children's conceptual development recorded?; Is there any over-reporting, like mark-lists that don't tell what knowledge or skills the children have worked on or acquired?

Action   The convenor produces forms for each teacher to add to every time they do a topic, to include all the elements that are seen as important by staff and clearly state the children's progress. For example the form may include name, year group, topic, core ATs worked on, other foundation subject knowledge and skills worked on, and intellectual and study skills demonstrated.

Folder for circulation   The current week's school news, courses, management issues and anything of general interest goes in here. Information for individual teachers about named children or which is confidential or in any way contentious, should not travel round the school in the folder.

The contents of the folder can be transferred to the staffroom noticeboard for further reference. The noticeboard could be divided not into subject headings (timetables, courses, trips, English, maths etc.) but into zones as shown in Figure 5.2.

Figure 5.2   Communication management: staffroom noticeboard layout

WHOLE SCHOOL PLANS AND INFORMATION				
TV and *Radio Times* and use, video, computers	Hall timetable, use of library, music room, field	Year timetable, closures etc.	Assembly plans	Whole school topics and other ventures (school garden etc.)

TEAM PLANS AND INFORMATION					
KEY STAGE 1			KEY STAGE 2		
Core	Foundation	Other	Core	Foundation	Other
Core Newsletters Resources Additions					

TEACHERS	CHILDREN
Courses/pay scales/union news	Book clubs/competitions/extra-curricular activities including sports and music

Communication outside school: formal and informal

Public relations   We have said that public relations are commonly part of the head's role. It seems that in future a school's public image may be even more important than in the past. The entrepreneurial and advertising skills of the head may do much to promote the 'successful' primary school of the future.

Parents   Parents and teachers are allies in the joint venture of securing the best possible learning opportunities for children. Parents' first concerns are with their own children. Teachers' concerns are for each child too. Any ill-feeling between teachers and parents is the result of misunderstanding. To avoid misunderstanding, communication is the key. Parents do not always know best, but their support of what is happening in school is vital. Teachers do not always know best either, but they have a better chance of meeting children's needs if there is mutual support between them and parents of the children they teach, and an open communication bridge across the school-home gap.

Governors   With the changes regarding the governing of schools, governors have an increasingly important job to do. Governors are powerful and their power can be to the school's advantage. The role of governor is to ensure that the school is achieving society's aims and objectives appropriately. Schools need therefore to maintain open communication and cordial relationships with governors. But governors have to respond to this through creative support for resource needs and curriculum development.

Other schools   Continuity and progression is a phrase used widely to support the introduction of the National Curriculum. It is indeed the case that it should now be easier to ensure continuity and progression through the schooling system. However, most communication between schools is still very formal. The possibilities of liaison will be increased to enable children to take up their studies in the secondary school where they left off in the primary sector. There are other ways in which communication between schools must now be extended; these have to do with teacher expertise and development needs, and assessment and moderation.

Groupings of children

Traditionally teachers have dealt with a class of pupils (commonly around 30 children) and from this base have arranged sub-groups and individual tasks. New patterns of organisation may emerge but for the present purpose we will assume that National Curriculum implementation will be under existing practices and expectations.

There is an argument, particularly amongst teachers of the youngest children, that a single class teacher is important. An adult who knows each child very well, and in whom they may want to confide, may be vital for emotional and social reasons. But there are powerful ways in which the opportunity to relate to other adults in an informal setting, maybe for particular purposes, enhances education. The benefits are these:

▶   Children are given some choice about relationships.

- Adults have the chance to share expertise with more children.

- Communication can be opened up throughout the school and teamwork is facilitated.

Approaches which aim to provide learning opportunities involving teaching that is less class-based, will result in important shifts of emphasis across the school. The main one is a move from passive to more active participation as shown below:

Passive	*Active*
Child as passive learner	Child as actively responsible for seeking learning
Child in fixed site	Child moves about the school, which may build confidence and independence
Teacher as subject specialist	Teacher as creator of learning opportunities
Teacher as generic expert	Teacher as pastoral carer with curriculum strengths
Teacher as independent	Teacher as member of a team.

Teacher and in-class groupings

If the school you work in chooses to keep traditional class-bound learning as pivotal, then you have little choice but to attempt to teach all the levels required, in all the subjects. There are teachers who will say they have been doing this all along. Always matching the teaching to each child is a difficult business. A common strategy is to adopt a model of the task, where all the children can 'have a go'; then performances are judged to be 'at the child's own level'. There is a case for this approach, especially when your attention is to be on an individual child; after all, you cannot focus on one child, and have six other different activities going on. On the whole, though, teaching must now be done in groups. In a class of 30, the spread of ability in different curriculum areas may be such that you need five or six groups; more than that and you are into individual work programmes; fewer and you are lumping together children with widely differing abilities and potential.

Ethnic, gender and ability bias and groupings

In setting up groupings, all teachers need to anticipate possible difficulties regarding the ethnic origin, gender and ability of the children. Humanitarian principles should govern your decisions about placing, for example, an 11-year-old boy in a group that is otherwise all girls, or a child with poor fine motor control amongst those who are highly skilled at practical tasks. There are no rules about groupings. A sensitive teacher can be far-sighted enough to manage them appropriately.

Summary

By way of a summary we have set out an example involving all the staff, where the management issues we have discussed are all represented.

Problem   Spelling. The school has only made ad hoc attempts to teach spelling in the past. The National Curriculum English AT in spelling does mean a more concerted effort must be made across the school in future.

Information collection   The English consultant collects strategies which staff currently use to teach spelling.

Reflection   All the teachers reflect on current practices, and study statements of attainment appropriate to the age group (and the relevant levels) they teach.

Action   All the teachers construct ways of enabling children to meet these statements of attainment. A whole-staff meeting is convened and all suggestions are aired. A school list of suggestions, appropriate to each level, is constructed and the teachers implement these. To monitor implementation and change the staff meet after, for example, half a term or a term to assess the children's progress. In the light of this, teaching and learning strategies can be modified and put into operation.

In brief, the management dilemmas are met like this:

Teamwork	Getting together over present and future strategies.
INSET	Reflection on present practices provokes new learning.
Leadership	The English consultant takes initiatives, collates and co-ordinates the team management exercise.
Time	The English consultant invests time in collecting teaching strategies from her colleagues and managing the whole exercise. Each member of staff needs a few minutes to write down their current practices and then there should be one meeting to arrive at future strategies.
Communication	This is in the English consultant's hands; the head is informed but not directing, and the communication with colleagues is full but to the point.
Groupings of children	Decided upon as part of future planning, with special provision made for children whose first language is not English.

In solving this problem the whole staff will have engaged in a management exercise. This model can be modified for other 'through school' management problems.

This chapter has, we hope, assured you that good management is within your grasp, and is not something that does not apply to the teaching profession.

CHAPTER 6

MANAGING THINGS

In providing for teaching and learning there are two dimensions which we need to look at; resourcing and managing resources. It is important to obtain resources which will support the work of the school and its National Curriculum delivery. But these resources will not of themselves enable appropriate learning to take place; they have to be managed. There are some ideas in Chapter 5 which apply to the management of things but there are some additional points to consider.

Optimal provision of resources occurs when schools and teaching teams enable access, at the right time, to what is appropriate for learning. The fundamentals underlying this delivery are to do with both accessing resources already available and selection of the appropriate new resources.

Accessing resources

Resources need to be available to individual teachers, to teaching teams, and centrally. With a network from the centre, through teams, to individuals, all teachers will have access to all school resources.

The crucial question in central resourcing is how accessible can/should material be? All items need to be appraised in terms of their intended users, safety, security and robustness. They also need to be viewed in terms of the degree to which they are amenable to pre-planning. For example, there is a difference in expecting teachers to predict when a tin of powder paint might run out and when a camera might be needed.

The key to optimising resource availability is to group things in terms of how far ahead you can predict their use. The shorter the time a teacher can safely predict their use then the nearer those resources need to be to him or her. Those items which can clearly be 'booked' well in advance can be centralised.

Classroom resources

All classrooms need to be equipped with basic material such as pencils, scissors, a stock of paper and so on. Depending on the architecture of the school and available space, classrooms may also have to store some art, science and design and technology materials. Many of these things will be of the yoghurt pot/egg box variety.

To make the most of class resources two things are required: ease of access and sensible rules. If you insist that children must get your permission to obtain any and every item, there are a set of clear consequences and implicit assumptions. You will have less continuous time for teaching, and children will have broken spells of application and extension. Obviously there are safety questions to be posed and answered but as far as possible it is desirable to share the responsibilities of access and return and care with your class.

Within the classroom you have flexibility of management. It may be helful if the children acquire some resource management skills. A mixed pattern of management may fit your style. For example, some resources can be 'given out', and stored and used by each individual child. Rulers, pencils and exercise books are among these. Some resources can be stored in an open class resource bank, on top of a cupboard or shelf, but in the classroom itself. These things may include a box of coloured pencils for each working group, scissors and glue. The class library fits this category too. 'New' stock and scarce resources like plain, graph and sugar paper can be placed in the classroom store. It is still accessible to children, but may only be so with your permission. Teacher resources can also be kept in the open classroom itself. If they are labelled as such, the children can still use them freely, but return them after use.

The study skills that serve children throughout their lives can be begun in the reception class. A child who can decide what they need to do a piece of work, can go and get those resources, use them properly and then put them away correctly and in good condition at the end of the task, is already a 'student'. If they can do it at the age of five, all their subsequent learning will be easier and they will assist their teacher's teaching.

Good classroom resource management means you can resource your lessons, in terms of every predictable outcome, before the lesson starts. You may well have experienced being interrupted in the middle of group work on a new concept by a child from another class carrying a note asking if you have got a box that will make a pin-hole camera, or tracing paper or green crayons. It wastes the time of the child carrying the message, your time in reading the note, even if you decide to write 'no' on it, and the time of the group whose attention you have now lost. They may, as a direct result of the interruption, lose the chance of mastering the new concept that day. In addition there is time lost by the teacher who wrote the note, and by the learners in her class.

On the other hand, if you alight on a rare or phenomenal resource, do give others the chance to use it, but let them incorporate it into their planning, as far as possible. It is infuriating to be asked to resource another teacher's teaching at a moment's notice. It is equally annoying to have others try to resource your teaching as it is happening. You may well have received, at some time, a message of the kind, 'There are kittens in 2B, would your class like to see them now?'

Team resources

Items such as schemes, age-related reading books and more sophisticated equipment should be centred on teams as far as possible. Such resources can be planned for and their need anticipated. As soon as a system which supports clear future planning is operating it will be possible to pool some of your resources.

Each team will need to keep a record of books, materials and equipment held, and this record must also be kept centrally. Access to resources must be defined. No member of a team should ever remove resources from the team source without agreement. Your desire to further your children's opportunities must not inhibit the opportunity for others. If a particular resource always seems to be in use and unavailable then this may be a good indication of a purchasing priority.

Central resources

Children and teachers throughout the school need access to the resources for the levels at which they are working. It is possible that this means more centralising of resources. Because teachers spend so much time face to face with the children, central resourcing has been unpopular in the past. Resources tend to be under-used if teachers have to go from one end of the building to the other to get them during their break. This applies especially when the resources may then prove unavailable. Strategies for making storage practical, and not a deterrent to use, need to be worked out. What will help is if you and your colleagues can be clear about what is best kept at the centre and what best looked after by teams. Central resources should include lists of resources and their locations, an attainment target level bank and, for example, copying facilities and cameras.

One way of increasing the attractiveness and efficient use of central resource banks is to make use of new technology. The construction of data bases of equipment and books which make use of key word indexes is well worthwhile.

Finally it is often the case that the outcomes of extended work by children and their teachers is worthy of placing in the central resource bank. The advent of word-processing and cheap desk-top publishing software now means that some of this work will be very well presented. These resources should not be ignored or forgotten even though their shelf life might be quite short.

Resource production

One way of sharing which has the virtue of economy is the development of resource banks which use school-produced items in tandem with commercial material. Class-produced books and models can be lent or given to other classes. Teacher-produced workcards and games can also be used throughout the school. They have to be made to a high standard, and well looked after. High standards of production and care can be maintained by teachers and instilled in children.

Copyright   In producing resource packs you must be careful about possible infringements of copyright. Whilst copyright laws are complex, there are some simple things to remember. Avoid photocopying sheets of music, large extracts from books, and showing videos without permission.

Choosing resources

Choosing written materials

Whilst there is now a greater variety of non-text materials available and in use in primary schools, it is true to say that the use of written materials is still at the heart of much of our work. For this reason we are concentrating on the evaluation of written materials in resource selection.

In evaluating resources it is necessary to be aware of the effect of the resource through the whole learning process. For example, if a school is aiming to develop children's abilities to organise their own study and use a resource-based learning approach, then materials which depend upon close teacher direction and timetabling will be unsuitable. Worse, if they were to be purchased they would undermine the overall integrity of the avowed approach of the school.

Over the last 25 years, there has been a glorious explosion in fictional books for children bringing with it an increasingly sophisticated appraisal of children's literature. The same cannot be said with regard to non-fictional books. It is still the case that books can be found in school which are supposed to support children in factual discovery, but are actually inaccurate, inappropriate or both. Adopting an evaluative approach will allow you to identify the inadequacies in the text and make informed choices.

Evaluating schemes

Within the limits of the budget a school may choose either a scheme-based approach or to use no all-through schemes. If the choice is scheme-based then the decisions you need to take are to do with which scheme/s, the cost, and the hidden costs.

Your aims and objectives will clearly influence your choice of a scheme. Also, physical characteristics such as size, print, readability and the use of illustrations will be factors in your choice. These aspects are dealt with in more detail below. The other major influence on your decision-making is going to be cost, and by this we do not mean the original outlay but the 'hidden' costs of a scheme. For example, if you need to purchase children's workbooks, what will be the recurrent cost per annum? And what other materials will need to be purchased to support the scheme? Depreciation together with running costs need to be added to the initial outlay in order to see the real costs of any scheme.

Evaluating texts

If you decide to have no all-through schemes, the only difference is the need to evaluate a range of written and other resources. So you need, here too, to be familiar with resource evaluation, purchasing needs and limits, and any in-service or other costs.

When purchasing texts your first priority must be to establish what elements of the National Curriculum will be supported. You will also have to evaluate the texts that you have in order to be clearer about purchasing needs.

There are a variety of ways in which written materials can be analysed but whatever the approach it must embrace:

a review of aims
compatibility with other school materials and systems
readability
physical characteristics.

Readability and other characteristics

Despite the fact that much of the material offered to children throughout their schooling is text-based, there is commonly a lack of sophisticated analysis of those materials. Research available indicates that the reading demands of many texts, including teacher-produced materials, is inappropriate for many of the children to whom it is offered. This mismatch is not only in matter of vocabulary but also the use of, for example, pictures, diagrams and statistical data. Also there is the need to examine texts for bias and prejudice in terms of stereotypes. The days of role casting in traditional ways and the exclusivity of middle class white children as the heroes and, less commonly, heroines of stories is not yet behind us.

Reading age   Whilst reading ages are useful to know about they do have severe limitations. They are snapshots, often posed in a way which children are not used to, and they generally say nothing about understanding. However, they are a useful broad guide when you are choosing materials. We have more to say about reading age in Chapter 9.

Readability measures   Readability measures have been developed more recently than reading age tests. There are, however, already a variety of them available. The intention in gauging readability is to indicate the demand of a piece of written material rather than the reading age of a child, although this is involved in the process. Readability measures are produced through the pooling of teacher judgements. These measures offer scores in terms of age and to that extent look like reading age scores. They are appraised in relation to the decisions of a large group of teachers on the reading demand of a given piece of material. Whilst readability measures are very useful they cannot and must not remove your responsibilities for making the final decisions about the appropriateness of texts. They cannot take account of children's interests and must not be used to limit the contact children have with new works and vocabulary. But they do have a place in your decision-making.

Pictures   Illustrations are important. We all like pictures, and particularly in non-fiction texts. The important items in evaluating illustrations are accuracy and relationship to the text, as well as aesthetic considerations (are they 'good' pictures?). These criteria apply to both fiction and non-fiction materials.

Pictures which illustrate statements in the text must correspond with what is stated. If a story talks about the hero/ine riding a tiger, then to see them on a lion is inappropriate and misleading. Although this may seem an exaggerated example, many books still contain this sort of inaccuracy which belittles the abilities and knowledge of children.

If an illustration is intended to support understanding it is usually, but not exclusively, to be found in non-fictional material. These pictures should be accurate and well reproduced, and should appear adjacent to the appropriate text.

Workcards Both commercially-produced and teacher-made workcards need critical examination for reading demand and concept complexity. The important question when examining workcards is whether or not they present tasks in an order which supports progression. A quick way to get at this for home-produced workcards is to keep a record of children's queries and mistakes. If a pattern emerges, it may be that a particular word or a conceptual leap in the workcard is the problem. You can then modify it. The same applies to bought-in workcards, but they can be hard to modify and a planned teaching intervention will be needed.

Choosing equipment

All equipment has a particular shelf life. But clearly some items, for example, paints and paper are consumables which need regular renewal. You will already have a wealth of experience in budgeting for consumables. It will, however, still be worth reviewing how you handle such things as exercise books against, say, ring-back files. It is beyond the scope of this book to give exhaustive advice on equipment selection but there are some basic questions and statements which will help.

The things to think about are:

> Does the price of a kit add up to more than the loose items?
> How often would a piece of equipment be used?
> How robust is the item?
> Can I make this myself?
> Will it actually do the job? (For example, the small microscopes often sold as being for children are actually hard for children to use because of the shake and size of the eyepiece.)

Summary: study skills and rules for resource use

If we tie together our two management strands, and put the people and resources together, it is possible to project schools moving towards a situation where:

▶ a resource database is on a central computer and can be accessed by teachers and children – it will give resource locations, lengths of loan and loan procedure

▶ children and teachers will be able to assemble the books, tapes, computer programs, workcards, apparatus etc. that they need before they start

▶ all resources will be stored in accessible places, on robust shelving or in strong boxes, meticulously labelled and looked after

▶ classes will be able to see from the computer database when the resources they need are on loan elsewhere

▶ teachers will train children to maintain a class record of resources in use (perhaps a class record on the door), so that resources do not stay 'out' when finished with.

When all this is in process, there will be a number of study and learning management skills being practised by teachers and children. These include resourcing learning, information retrieval, and accessing information from a database. There will also evolve a system of rules to enable maximum access and use of resources. This is good resource management.

Teachers in small schools may feel this grand system does not apply to them. However, the same broad model can be applied in a two-teacher school; you will still need to store, access and manage. In fact such a system could operate between schools, especially where they become federated. To resource the National Curriculum may be difficult for some schools and resource management between schools may be the only way to achieve it.

MANAGING CHANGE

The National Curriculum prescribes curriculum content and assessment. You have to plan and manage your critical path through to your version of National Curriculum delivery. Given that you know more or less where you are heading and you can establish where you are now, then the path you choose to take is the path of change. Whether or not that path has severe gradients with many bends and dead ends, or is fairly smooth and direct, will depend on your ability to manage its progressive construction.

This chapter has two sections. The first sets out the steps in implementing school change. In the second section we look at classroom change within the context of a whole-school plan.

Innovation and change: a problematic area

There are two major and often opposing issues which face all institutions, whether they be schools or businesses: they are the need to maintain current activity and the need to innovate and change. The reason that they are in opposition is that system maintenance must resist change; its job is to minimise disruption and to keep day-to-day work on an even keel. For innovation and change to take place systems must be developed or even removed and replaced. Eric Hoyle expresses this tension very well:

> 66 *Curriculum innovation requires change in the internal organisation of the school. Change in the internal organisation of the school is a major innovation.* 99
>
> Harris, A. *et al* (eds), *Curriculum Innovation* (Croom Helm, 1975)

However, knowing this is not much help except that it does alert us to the need to understand our own situations in order to best overcome obstacles. Without this understanding and an appreciation that genuine innovation needs time to take root, our plans are likely to be unrealistic.

Whole-school change

In a real sense change is what education is all about. We all aim to bring about changes in children in terms of their knowledge, skills and behaviour. Transferring this sort of ambition to ourselves and our colleagues is often problematic. There are always many good reasons for not changing! As we have already emphasised in this section the most important factor is the people. They, together with their resource support are what you need to put at the heart of your planning process. This applies whether you are producing the school development plan or innovating in your classroom.

The first step in bringing about change is to draw up a logical set of plans which will offer aims and deadlines. As deadlines are reached the particular achievements should inform and refine your initial plan.

One way of approaching the task in hand is to take the following steps:

1 *Describe in detail how you would wish your school to look in five years time.* This description should be as full as you can make it and needs time and a consideration of the views of others. In addition to curriculum matters it should include statements on organisation.

2 *Contrast your picture of five years hence with the current situation.* What is important here is to itemise those things which are absent, those which require modification and those which you will have to protect. It is easy to forget that concentrating your efforts on new skills or concerns may actually undermine current strengths. Things missing or requiring change need to be analysed to clarify what they really are to do with. You can then group issues together and reduce the length of the list.

3 *Prioritise the groupings and allocate a notional deadline for the achievement of change.* The way to approach this is to work out a flow chart which should indicate which group or set of items must be achieved before related sets can be tackled. Even if this means breaking a group down into stages then still persist with the approach. The more detailed the planning is at this stage the better.

4 *Draw up a first-year plan which embraces those things which you need to achieve first.* At this point separate out personal/professional needs from resource needs.

Personal/professional needs

1 *Determine your/colleagues' needs in relation to the overall plan.* Schools have experience in drawing up INSET needs and allocating budgets to staff development initiatives. The one possible difficulty that may arise is how to use this experience in the context of a long-term plan. Commonly schools have given more emphasis to the short-term needs of colleagues and the school. With the advent of the National Curriculum it will be necessary to take the longer view in order to ensure that the INSET stepping stones are in the right place and sequence.

2 *List the ways in which people's needs may be met and prioritise them.* The possibilities range from very short, often whole-staff and school-based INSET to long part-time courses which are commonly associated with awards. Other initiatives might include work experience in industry, secondment to LEAs or other bodies, research and development activities and validating your own INSET course with a local HE institution. There are a wide variety of ways of offering yourself and your colleagues development opportunities some of which are, as yet, not commonly experienced. Use your governors from outside the education sector as contributors of ideas. When the list is completed compare it with your resource list, especially with regard to finance.

3 a) *Draw up a first-year staff development rota for individuals.*   b) *Draw up a first-year whole-staff development calendar.* In doing these things you should also indicate opportunities coming up for yourself and colleagues beyond year 1. This is necessary for the positive encouragement of those not covered in the first sweep.

4 *At the end of year 1 appraise progress in relation to your five-year plan and generate the year 2 priorities.* It is the case that there are always unforeseen problems and possibilities. You may even achieve more than you might have hoped. It is also the case that your five-year plan may need modification, but changes should not be major ones if your initial planning was detailed enough.

Resource plans

1 *Determine the resourcing needs.* These should be for both curriculum and staff development.

2 *List which resources you have; you can readily obtain; appear impossible to get.* The difficulty here is going to be financial. However, there are sources of support that you may not yet have tapped and with local financial management it is necessary to explore new avenues and new ways of sharing. Again make use of your governors. Look at partnerships with other schools. Don't forget barter!

3 *Draw up and initiate a first-year resource acquisition plan.*

4 *Regularly review progress in both the development and resources first-year plans.* At the end of the year generate year 2 initiatives and modify the five-year plan in the light of progress made.

For the purpose of a school development plan all of these planning steps need to be taken by a staff team. Every member of the team needs to understand and contribute to the five-year plan and have a role in developing each stage and obtaining resources.

In drawing up such plans it is vital that you take close account of those things which might inhibit their development. There are two major contributors to the resistance to change. They are people and resources.

Understanding resistance to change: people

There are two main reasons why people resist change; experience and security.

a) Experience

We are qualified and have obtained our right to teach through many years of schooling and a period of higher education. Throughout this process we have gained and refined a number of beliefs and theories about what constitutes sound classroom and school practice. In order for us to initiate change or to be changed in our views it is necessary for there to be good reasons. These reasons must be well thought out and of sufficient substance to cause us to revise our belief systems. Changing one's mind on important issues is no light undertaking. Whilst legislation requires us to implement a National Curriculum this will not be delivered successfully until experienced teachers make the content, if not the spirit of it, their own and thereby give it credibility. This is why the National Curriculum Council is devoting resources to in-service and information materials.

Our experience in schools is another factor. The range of experience of different school organisations, colleagues, locations and sizes will all contribute to the range of possible responses we can offer to curriculum development.

b) Security

There are several connected issues which relate to our sense of well-being in our professional activities. The major ones are status, self-confidence and personal learning style.

Status   We are all status conscious. Status is particularly important in the field of education because the whole system depends on respect. Respect in schools is generally based upon a combination of personal characteristics and role. In achieving promotion we all expect to attain higher status in the eyes of our colleagues. The fact that the status of teachers in society is not always what we would wish does not affect that expectation, except to accentuate it within the profession.

Promotion is based upon experience and achievements. It is associated, usually, with your 'track record'. This is obviously about the past. Having gained promotion it is likely that this 'track record' will keep you running in the same sort of race under similar conditions. But when the conditions and/or rules change they are difficult to accommodate. Whilst high status brings greater scope for influencing change it also brings greater accountability. The common-sense statement that the younger members of the profession are more able to change is not to do with age. It is to do with the fact that they usually do not have hard-earned status positions to protect.

Self-confidence   This is not a constant, although it is true to say that some people seem to be more confident generally than others. But appearances can deceive. It is always worth reminding yourself that you can perform very well in certain circumstances and that other people are also under-confident when faced with new situations. In recalling times, places and activities in which you are confident you need to be attempting to transfer that feeling to the new demands, not using them to try and turn a new situation into something familiar.

Learning style   We know that children differ in their approaches to learning and we know that different teaching approaches affect children in different ways. But seldom do we use this knowledge, together with the personal knowledge we have of our own learning preferences and approaches to inform the strategies we can adopt to promote staff development. One of the reasons that some colleagues do not undertake regular INSET willingly may be to do with how these INSET opportunities are presented. Active learning sessions may be problematic for some as lectures may be for others. Distance learning with the flexibility it offers in day to day terms may be attractive to one person and anathema to another.

Responding to resistance In developing your response to people's resistance to change it is important to keep in mind the personal priorities and fears that colleagues may have. You may need help. There are times when we all need an outsider to act as a catalyst for change. Outsiders can be convenient whipping boys as well as offering new ways of viewing a familiar problem. The thorough, and enjoyable, dissection of the presenter after an in-service day can serve a very useful purpose. Not only does it act as a safety valve but the fact of the conversation will often throw up some new thoughts and offer the opportunity for a number of subtle but important changes of perspective.

Understanding resistance to change: resources

There is not enough money to support the purchase of materials and equipment and to underwrite staff and whole-curriculum development. Often schools are flooded with resources tailored to the plans of 15 or more years ago. It is tempting to use texts and schemes beyond their real shelf life and to defer decision-making about possible replacements or even alternatives. This temptation is fuelled by tight budgets and over-full resource agendas. There is no doubt that National Curriculum implementation means that you are going to have to justify retention of some resources rather than having to justify their replacement. Wise choices, phased purchase, sharing, begging and borrowing are some ways to offset an inadequate budget and obsolete equipment.

Classroom change

The planning process for classroom change is the same as for a whole-school plan, and it is within the context of that plan that you can construct a year forecast. If we list the processes in planning, they run like this:

► Describe in detail what you hope to have achieved within the school year.

► Compare your proposals with the situation in the class now.

► List your intentions in order of priority, and set time limits.

► Decide, and write down, what you want to achieve in the autumn term.

► Determine your own needs in relation to your plan, and devise your own development programme.

► List the resources you need, and how you can access them.

► Work out how you will manage the resources to carry through your plan.

► Review your plan and outcomes often and set modified targets each term.

Summary

If you want to bring about change you need to analyse the current situation in order to really understand what you are proposing to move from. The two most important elements to examine are curriculum delivery and the climate of operation within the school. Both should be looked at in relation to the demands of National Curriculum and assessment. People are at the heart of the system and they need to be considered at all levels and stages of implementation and change. Resources provide some of the important raw materials for fuelling teaching and learning and they need careful evaluation and management. In examining innovation and change you should take account of the need for the following:

> Support from governors, colleagues and your LEA
> A high degree of co-ordination
> Staff development capacity
> Clear and well thought out structures and organisation
> Good communication and co-operative working
> A recognition of the demands on colleagues
> Clear forward planning.

D EVALUATION AND ASSESSMENT

This section is about approaches to evaluation which will be important in developing informed judgements about childrens' progress through the National Curriculum. The aims are to give support in:

▶ collecting information in the school and classroom

▶ understanding tests and testing

▶ keeping records

▶ making judgements.

Introduction

There are many and various calls on a teacher's time. It is often the case that evaluation and assessment are seen as additional burdens on already overburdened teachers. But the National Curriculum working parties see the necessity of putting much of the evaluation, monitoring, and assessment demands of the National Curriculum into teachers' individual and collective hands.

In final documents relating to the National Curriculum, much is said about the fact that teachers must do assessment, and the keeping of clear records is tied to this requirement. Little, however, is said about evaluation.

Evaluation

Evaluation is the term used for finding out about, judging, and acting upon the process of learning in your classroom. We think that, after interaction with children, evaluation is the second most important part of a teacher's role. Indeed, the quality of interaction with children crucially depends upon the appropriateness and efficiency of the teacher's prior evaluation, and the sensitivity of the teacher.

Evaluation is difficult to do for two reasons. The first is that the information available in a classroom is so varied and complex. The second is the need to work out the relative importance of pieces of information. Assessment and record keeping are vital elements of evaluation. But test results alone will not enable you to adequately gauge children's progress through the levels of the

National Curriculum. Your repertoire will extend from your sensitivity and perception, through a range of tools and techniques, to informed judgements and appropriate actions. In order to be an evaluator of your own classroom, you must grapple with your concerns about the following:

▶ Your own subjectivity

▶ The complexity of the information

▶ The means by which the information may be collected

▶ Ways of implementing the outcomes of evaluation.

Assessment

Assessment is that part of evaluation in which you are investigating children's, and your own, learning in relation to a fixed task. Examples of assessment are marking children's work, giving pencil and paper tests, giving a problem-solving activity with a view to establishing what a child has learned about a particular activity, and working through a test exercise in, for example, computer keyboard skills, yourself.

The assessment arrangements within the National Curriculum provide for two kinds of assessment, internal and external. Internal assessments will have to support continuity and progression. These include, for example, teacher assessments, reading age tests, and mathematics graded workbooks. External assessments will locate individuals in relation to criteria set locally and nationally. The overall pattern of the outcomes of these assessments will be used to place schools' achievements in relation to other schools. These assessments will include SATs.

However, whilst external assessment will be important, it is essential to maintain and develop the quality of internal assessments, in order to give a full picture of children's progress. The writers of the documents relating to the National Curriculum are unequivocal in their insistence on the importance of teacher assessment to support the external kind.

> **❝** *Teachers' own assessments are an essential part of the system. They will be able to cover aspects of performance not readily testable by conventional means, and more generally will ensure a place in the assessments for rounded qualitative judgements.* **❞** (para.6.5)

> **❝** *Teachers will ... be expected to keep a record of pupils' progress in relation to each attainment target: this will provide a general basis for planning their work.* **❞** (para. 6.9)

> **❝** *Teachers' records which contribute to the overall formal assessments at ages 7, 11, 14 and 16 should be of real value in securing improvements in continuity and progression, particularly when pupils change schools.* **❞** (para. 6.10)

> DES, *National Curriculum: from Policy to Practice*

In order to meet the needs of National Curriculum it will be necessary for you to have a repertoire of assessment techniques at your finger tips. SATs will be only one element in the school and classroom assessment practice. All of the outcomes of assessment need to be related to all of the other processes in school through evaluation.

Record keeping

The natural adjunct for assessment is the keeping of records. It is also a natural requirement for and consequence of evaluation. Teachers' records range from the idiosyncratic shorthand, through school internal systems, to local and national records, which share common descriptions and assume shared understandings.

Records aid evaluation and assessment by summarising your thinking and supporting your memory. First-rate record keeping will actually help to enhance your creativity and illuminate your observations of the children's learning. Whilst we will not claim that good record keeping improves the memory, it will supplement what you can remember, however good your memory.

Evaluation, assessment and record keeping

If you picture evaluation as being a means of mapping the classroom, then assessment is to do with the routes on that map. Assessing involves you in looking at the route and at the milestones along the route. Developing the metaphor further, we might relate assessment to road building programmes, and evaluation to a policy for the whole environment. Environment policies are hard to manage, road building is easier. That is to say, evaluation is much more difficult than assessment. Without an environment policy the roads may be inappropriately built. Without evaluation, assessments do not measure what you hoped. And without accurate and full record keeping you will not be able to recall where you have been and where you might be moving to next.

CHAPTER
8
EVALUATION

The issues of evaluation and assessment which come up in the National Curriculum are not new. What is new is the emphasis on both standardised and teacher assessments, and their combination. To fully respond to the demands of the assessment arrangements, and develop rounded appraisal systems, all teachers will need to become evaluators in their own classrooms and schools.

This chapter is about 'doing' evaluation. There are three major requisites if you are to become a teacher-evaluator: firstly, a way of visualising the context in which you are operating; secondly, knowledge of ways of collecting information; and finally, a willingness to really use your informed judgements for development purposes. Ways into the first two are offered in this chapter, the third will come through personal application of these.

Starting evaluation

To begin an evaluative investigation a problem must be recognised. For example: 'In my view, Joan's behaviour around school is unruly. Are my perceptions shared by colleagues?' 'How did I perform in class last Tuesday?' 'Why did Mahmud learn from that session and not Michael?' 'How can we extend the use the children make of the school non-fiction library?'

A way of stating the continuing process that is needed is:

> **Sensing of issues**
> **Pinpointing of problems**
> **Information collection and analysis**
> **Reflection and judgement**
> **Action and monitoring**
> **Location of changes**

and then **SPIRAL** again!

Evaluating in the classroom

In isolating a dilemma or problem, or pointing up an area for evaluation, three major elements need to be considered. They are the child, the teacher and the task.

These can be arranged as a triangle (Figure 8.1).

Figure 8.1   Starting points for evaluation

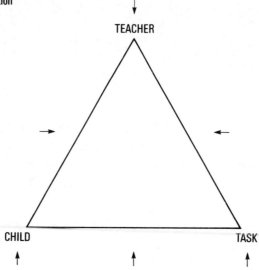

There are six possible starting points for an investigation.

> Teacher
> Child
> Task
> Teacher ↔ child
> Child ↔ task
> Teacher ↔ task

To illustrate how these starting points can be useful, here are some examples. The different presentations reflect different problems, but they are all underpinned by the **SPIRAL** approach and the triangle model.

Starting point: the teacher

Problem   How successful was I in preparing the class for the TV programme 'Watch'? Were there points I didn't cover? How can I tell?

Information collection   I decided to look at what happened before, during and after the programme.

What I did before the programme:
> Read teachers' notes
> Read appropriate sections of children's library books
> Consulted staff library
> Listed key concepts.

Activities in the class before the programme:

> Arranged display of books
> Class discussion
> Discovered children's present knowledge
> Pointed out appropriate sections of books to children as a class
> Encouraged children to use display.

What happened during the programme?

> Watched with the children
> Took notes – key concepts' observed children's behaviour

What happened after the programme?

> Feedback from the children
> Listed the misunderstandings.

Reflection and action   I took action for the four programmes that followed in the 'Watch' series. I attempted all that I had been doing before but undertook some additional work. Upon reflection I felt I could improve the preparation by:

► priming myself well ahead, not the week before

► planning that the programme fits the term's activities and come at the appropriate time in the term

► introducing the key concepts (perhaps in other contexts) before the programme.

Commentary

We think that the teacher should also consider whether:

► more use should be made of video

► less emphasis should be placed on watching all the programmes in a series

► the emphasis should shift from pupil passivity to pupil activity before as well as after the programmes.

Starting point: the child

Problem   Gary is inattentive and disrupts the work of others in his group some of the time each week. Why?

Information collection   Teacher records Gary's behaviour problem over two weeks as shown in Figure 8.2. This is an attempt to track Gary's problem to a time of day or week, or trace links with his or others' assigned activities.

Figure 8.2   Problem behaviour record 1

NAME:

DAY	TIME	What group were assigned to do	What rest of class was assigned	Description of problem behaviour	Action by teacher if any

Reflection   The teacher's records show that Gary behaves most inappropriately when the group are working on practical tasks with little supervision. In these sessions he does very little practical work, interrupting others' efforts to use the resources. His recording is untidy and incomplete. The teacher decides to assist Gary by giving him a sense of achievement. She does this by helping Gary to make a good start on the task and improve his recording.

Action   Here are some strategies she can adopt to enhance Gary's prospects:

▶ After group introduction help Gary get started by introducing the task again if necessary.

▶ Set him work as an individual among the group.

▶ Make his tasks more 'closed' and shorter.

▶ Give him more regular checks and reinforcement than other members of the group.

▶ When bringing together the group's work allow Gary a chance to contribute.

▶ Praise the improvement in his efforts.

The teacher adopts these strategies for several 'open' learning sessions and keeps records as shown in Figure 8.3. The teacher then reviews the tasks during which Gary behaves appropriately and achieves success. The intention is to enable Gary to work towards behaving appropriately in more and more open learning tasks. As this will take time, the teacher decides to implement change over two terms. To manage this the following strategies may be appropriate:

Figure 8.3   Problem behaviour record 2

TOPIC/SUBJECT: **GROUP:**

Group tasks	Gary's tasks	Gary's behaviour	Gary's achievements	Teacher comments

▶ Keep Gary on shorter, more structured tasks until his behaviour is not disruptive to others. He will then achieve and gain confidence.

▶ Let Gary demonstrate his new learning to another child and for some short tasks work with that child.

▶ Gradually give Gary a little less supervision and slightly longer tasks.

▶ Revert to structured work when it is not possible to monitor Gary. Don't let him relapse.

Commentary

The thrust of teacher effort has been to change Gary's work tasks and work style temporarily, in order to enhance his motivation and confidence. The hope is that he will want to get on and work. If these strategies prove unsuccessful it may be appropriate to withdraw Gary from the group and devise a different learning programme for him. But he will still need to have full access to the National Curriculum.

Starting point: the task

Problem   Following a group learning session on electrical circuit making, children were asked to record their discoveries. All but one sought teacher help with recording. How can their skills be improved?

Information collection and reflection   Teacher recalls that the children:

- ▶ made guesses rather than deductions
- ▶ found it hard to focus on which information to record
- ▶ recorded their observations in unsystematic fashion
- ▶ asked for help that indicated that they are unclear about some of the rules of work in science. They did not show they knew that scientific method requires that ideas are tested through experiment. Also they failed to appreciate that in an experiment things are varied in a controlled way and detailed notes and records of changes and observations are necessary.

Action   The teacher decides to engage the group in a discussion about the nature of science. Key words from the children can be recorded on a large sheet of paper or a blackboard. Words might include: discovery, experiment, results, finding out, idea, happenings, chance, problem, findings, probability, expectation. From their discussion children can be helped to understand logical approaches to the problem.

As a group, look at all the children's results. Teacher asks what are the ways that the results could be made easy to read and understand. 'Can we link like with like?' 'Can we list?' 'Can the results be tabulated?' As a group devise a number of different ways of recording findings.

The children can then have a go at a similar problem or choose one of their own devising. They can tackle the recording. A group feedback session follows, so that the children may learn from one another.

Commentary

Teacher's planned change must be to give the group a chance to record many kinds of data in various ways. Work may result in a resource book made by the children, called 'In the Charts', or a group work display.

One of the most difficult tasks for teachers is to raise individual standards. It is tempting, given the pressure of classroom work, to accept children's work as being 'good enough'. National Curriculum directives make it possible to adopt a rigorous approach and help children to see that quality recording, discussion and planning are necessary for their own learning.

Starting point: the teacher–the child

Problem   The class do not respond to open questions and discussion.

Information collection   The teacher collates the following information relating to the class: composition; seating arrangements; friendship groups; who are the natural leaders; who is articulate; age, sex and ethnic distribution.

Reflection   Teacher reflects on his or her own style. Is he or she too forceful and uncompromising, or too diffident? How does he or she handle the children's expressions of opinion and the whole idea of children talking?

Action   In the teacher's view it seemed the following ideas might help:

▶ Make a minor change in seating for oral work.

▶ Establish an 'oral tradition', with time each day for talk.

▶ Provide a range of speaking experiences, including paired discussion, interviews, role play, drama, puppets, group discussion, reported feedback from groups and poetry reading.

▶ Explain the principles of democracy and debate so that minority views can be expressed.

▶ Find out what the children want to talk about.

▶ Give every child a chance to speak.

Commentary

Ways of monitoring what goes on might include noting how often each child speaks out, in what setting, and in response to what issues. Further reflection may result in the recomposition of groups. For example, remove the child who constantly 'holds the floor' or make groups single sex. Another outcome may be the establishment of oral work in some curriculum areas where the children have had the idea that they may not talk. A final outcome may be that the children demonstrate, through talking more, that they need to learn even more sophisticated speaking and listening skills.

Starting point: the child–the task

Problem   Joseph is a boy with considerable ability who persistently underperforms in recording a structured English exercise. For this work members of his group choose from a pack of cards, an illustrated 'short story' card. They are expected to read the story, ask themselves the questions beneath it, choose one of the suggested options for story-writing and write their own story.

Information collection   Teacher observes Joseph's attack on the task and the way he does the task. She discusses with him his choice of card and his written work, and explores with him his personal interests and reading choices. He names five favourite books, and five things he likes doing outside school.

Reflection   On reflection teacher decides that Joseph may respond better to non-fiction information.

Action   Teacher acts on this by suggesting a factual idea prompted by a card. He is shown how to resource his work and how to structure his writing. For example, the card has a story about hot air balloons. Options include, 'Would you like to go ballooning? What would it be like?' Joseph's task is to read the story and the options; look in the library for books on balloons, ballooning, and 'in the air'; choose two; read them; and write a report of a hot air balloon ride or race.

Commentary

Though the introduction of a factual element in Joseph's work may have increased his motivation and output, there may be other reasons for his improvement, when faced with what seems a more challenging task. He may be enlivened by the challenge itself. This idea could be tested by continuing to give Joseph more challenging work, and in other areas of the curriculum. He will then have the chance to demonstrate exceptional skills he may have which require an individually-based work programme.

Starting point: teacher–task

Problem   The teacher works in a school where topics are decided 'collectively' and is assigned one which must be done, but seems irrelevant or arbitrary.

Information collection and reflection   The teacher records his or her own feelings in order to identify the roots of the antipathy. He or she does this by listing the advantages and disadvantages of doing this assigned topic. This list embraces not just the educational pros and cons but also the personal demands and those involving other staff.

The teacher then records the collective thinking which has led to the topic suggestion, and how it is linked to the work of other classes, if at all. A link may lead into an investigation of the topic through areas that are of interest to the class and teacher.

Action   The outcomes of these exercises is the development of new topic titles for use with the children whilst still meeting the demands of the school policy. These new titles offer the teacher more flexibility whilst still embracing the same sorts of knowledge, concepts, skills and attitudes as the original title.

If self-evaluation does not help, the teacher can team up with a colleague and they can plan a linking topic together. The evaluation exercise is then one of the team project and how to operate it.

Commentary

New topic titles can change the perspective of both teacher and children. For example, 'Monsters' takes on real life appeal if you look at mini-beasts under a magnifier, 'Smile' sounds more lively than 'Teeth', and 'Why is the sky blue?' could provoke more learning than 'Colour' or 'Space'. 'Held captive' is provocative while 'Zoos' may not be.

It is vital that, in this kind of evaluation, the teacher uses all the available resources in the school, that is, the school library, the staff library, his or her colleagues and most importantly, the children.

Techniques

There are many ways in which information for evaluation purposes can be collected. We have made a selection from these using two criteria: they work, and they are practicable for busy teachers and Heads. Each method is described with some suggestions for use or illustrative material. The techniques discussed are:

> Diaries
> Observation
> Audio recording
> Asking questions
> Group discussion.

Diaries

A very good way of gathering information about your own practice is to keep a diary. There are two main ways of using a diary: as a general information and issues analysis tool, or a way of collecting information on a particular child, task, or event. In both cases the same practices should apply.

Decide upon a period of time for keeping the diary. This period of time must relate to what you are going to use your diary for. If you are focusing on a particular sort of lesson then you will need to keep a diary over some weeks for just those lessons. If for an overview, then one week in which notes are kept every day may suffice. In either case, when you have completed your diary, put it away for a week. Then read it. You will find that you write better than you thought, and that unanticipated issues leap out of the page. It does not really matter whether you write full blown prose or short notes. What is important is that you have a record made by you and open to interpretation by you.

The evaluation example with the child as a starting point, on pp. 91–3, is an example of a diary.

Observation

Observing teaching is a common approach for researchers in classrooms. Many checklists and schedules have been produced to assist observers in this task. However, here we are concerned with the use of observation by teachers. There are situations in which it is possible to get feedback on your teaching, for example if you work with teacher trainers and their students, or have a trusted colleague in school or on an in-service course with you, but generally you are on your own. In that situation observation must be to do with the children in your class.

The main things to observe are the children's talk and behaviour. Whilst teachers are 'observing' these things all of the time, it is useful to make periodic formal observations. The National Curriculum programmes of study in areas such as speaking and listening back up this need. In order to formalise some of your observation rather than rely on day-to-day non-formal observation it is necessary to plan when and how you will observe.

The evaluation example on pp. 94–5 with teacher–child as starting point contains observation of the children.

Audio recording

In the busy atmosphere of the classroom it is often difficult to closely evaluate children's learning difficulties. It is easy to know when children do not understand, but it is harder to diagnose the nature of the problem. Using a cassette tape recorder whilst working with a group can be of great help in disclosing children's approaches, thoughts and misunderstandings. Listening to a tape away from the classroom will immediately allow you to hear more of the exchanges rather than just the ones on which you were concentrating at the time. What children say will also tell you a lot about their skills in communication within a group.

Another way of using audio recording is to allow children to record and listen to their own work. It is striking how children start to be critical and self-correcting when put into this situation. Such work can be built into your teaching programme. You can use it for reading practice. You can have a class or group topic presented in part as a slide tape or book tape (this will also add to the resources of the school). Whilst the value of the recording as a stimulus to learning is clear, there is also the possibility of your obtaining a good evaluative outcome if you take time away from the class to listen to the tapes.

In using audio tape there are two words of caution. Do be conscious of the need to have a good quality microphone and allow children to use headphones when working alone. It is profitable on occasions to transcribe some of the conversations onto paper as it allows you to go backwards and forwards over a passage. However, transcription does take a long time so be certain that it is necessary, before you start.

Asking questions

There are two ways of trying to get answers to questions, through talk and on paper. Talking and listening is conversation. You can record questions and answers on paper or tape; this is an interview. The following approaches can be useful to you.

Conversations Conversations are the starting points for all educational theories. You are already a conversationalist. But it is possible to use a conversational approach as an evaluation tool. We are all aware of those conversations where we have come away with new insights, or a suspicion of a hidden message, or both. An evaluation conversation is just like that. It is your attempt to gather information informally, but in a planned and purposeful way. It is rather like an informal interview but important nonetheless.

Interviews Interviews are formalised conversations. Decide beforehand exactly what you want to find out. Write down a form of words. Those TV interviews that look relaxed and impromptu are the result of research, carefully worded questions, rehearsal and editing. If you are well prepared and know what you want to investigate (not what you want to confirm or disprove!) then there is a good chance colleagues or children will tell you, if they know. You do have to be careful that your approach and question wording is not biased, and bear in mind that children (and colleagues sometimes) are eager to please, and will try to fit in with what they think you want to hear.

Questionnaires Questionnaires are part of the experience of teachers and children, but not usually in relation to evaluation. There are lots of times when classes are involved in surveying opinions in the school in order to, say, construct block graphs of 'My favourite . . .' or 'I would like schools to be . . .'. These are statistical exercises and involve children in constructing questions on paper, posing those questions, and analysing responses. These are the same skills needed in questionnaire design and analysis. You can use questionnaires to help your own and children's evaluations. You or the children, or both, could write some questions on work completed, and all of the class could answer these questions on a scale from, say, very enjoyable to positively disliked. One interesting variation on this is to ask a question and then give children a six-point scale set out thus:

> YES!　　Yes　　yes　　no　　No　　NO!

Most of the value of using questionnaires in the classroom is the support it gives to children developing their own evaluative skills and opinions. It is, of course, possible to use questionnaires with colleagues, but still keep them simple and avoid reading too much into the responses. An example of such a simple questionnaire would be to ask colleagues to rank areas in need of current development, and then indicate the degree of importance within the ranking.

Group discussion

We are all used to group discussion. The structure tends to revolve around the chair and the articulate contributor. There are other ways of setting up discussions and these can be used profitably in agenda creation and evaluation exercises.

Maps   The use of topic webs by teachers in their planning can be adapted in order to gain insights into children's prior knowledge and new learning. The procedure is to generate key words which characterise and/or describe a topic. This can be done individually or through group discussions. Every child then has to draw a web of the topic using the key words, and any they can add, in order to offer a guide to someone who knew nothing about the topic. Your perusal of these 'maps' will provide much useful material on individual children and their achievements and next steps.

This 'brain storming' approach also has its place with colleagues. It is a very good way of developing agenda material for a staff meeting or the planning or identification of in-service provision, or for aspects of a school development plan.

Snowball   One technique, often called 'snowball' for reasons which will become obvious, supports all members of the group making a contribution. To run such a discussion you:

▶ ask all members to write down their thoughts on a chosen topic or issue, individually and without talking to each other

▶ get individuals in pairs to discuss their notes and agree a combined contribution

▶ then make groups of four from the pairs and so on.

Clearly there are limits to the eventual group size, eight is a good final number, and you will have to play around with numbers (maybe threes not pairs at the first stage). By the end of the cycle everyone will have contributed and the identification of main points will be well advanced. This technique is economical with time and works well with children as well as colleagues.

Nominal group technique   In this approach you ask all members to make short notes about the chosen topic, again without discussion. In this case the topic should be polarised. For example, 'What I like or do not like about school' or 'The strengths and weaknesses of our organisation'. It is a good idea to have the group sitting in a horseshoe rather than behind each other. You will need a scribe, or do the writing yourself, and you will need a blackboard, overhead transparency, or paper pinned up. Ask each member in turn to give you one item from their list and the scribe writes this up. It is important that no one is allowed to question the item, except for clarification of meaning. In other words no item is to be classified as 'wrong' or 'unsuitable'. Continue around the horseshoe taking one item at a time. After the first complete sweep return to the first person and ask for a second item which has not yet appeared. Continue with this process until no one has any more items to contribute. Repeat the exercise for the negative part of the question. You now have a lot of data. There are various ways of using this data. You could:

▶ use it for an agenda for a subsequent discussion

▶ get members to work in twos or threes grouping the data to try and isolate the major points

▶ allow members to select items which particularly interest them for a more general discussion.

One of the virtues of these techniques is novelty, so do not use them too often. They also permit everyone to contribute, without having to stand up and formally 'take the floor'.

Summary

Evaluation will enhance your sense of professionalism and help you to be more efficient and effective. Evaluation builds on the common sense decisions you make every day about your own work, your class and your school.

▶ Evaluations are informed judgements. The outcomes of evaluation are often ways of understanding and ameliorating dilemmas and problems.

▶ Evaluation is about change and potential. The conclusion of an evaluation exercise marks the point at which you can act to improve what happens in the next session or week or term.

▶ Evaluation colours the future. It is a starting point for your next steps in the education of yourself and your pupils.

▶ Evaluation is the springboard for teaching and learning. Get on and do it and you will manage the National Curriculum even better than you hoped.

CHAPTER 9

ASSESSMENT AND TESTING

Assessment and the National Curriculum

Children's attainment in relation to the National Curriculum will be compiled from teachers' assessments and some national arrangements called standard assessment tasks (SATs). The National Curriculum puts the assessment into your hands, both through your formative (continuous) assessment of children's progress, and through summative assessment at key stages.

Formative assessment

Formative or continuous assessment is what you record at regular (but not necessarily equal) intervals, about the children's work. For example, you mark every piece of English written work that Freddie does, but every two weeks you record the kinds of successes he has and the kinds of mistakes he makes. Over time, the record will give the amount and directions of Freddie's progress. This kind of assessment is regular, takes place over time, and is cumulative.

Summative assessment

Summative assessment takes place at the end of a period of time or at the completion of a particular area of learning. It has a meaning and importance outside the classroom, for example, within the whole school, to other schools, to parents and to employers. The audience are assumed to have some understanding of the routes that led to the assessment task, its content, and the time in the school year or the age of the children when it is done. Sometimes these assessments are called external. End-of-term exams, public examinations and SATs fall into this category.

How the national assessment system is being developed

The development of SATs is being undertaken under the auspices of SEAC who, for key stage 1, have asked three organisations to develop SATs and prepare guidance for teachers. The initial work was done by a working group called the Task Group on Assessment and Testing (TGAT). We have already mentioned this group in Chapter 2.

The Task Group on Assessment and Testing faced a pretty formidable task. They put it like this:

> **❝** *We are required to propose a national assessment system which enhances teaching and learning without any increase in the calls on teachers' and pupils' time for activities which do not directly promote learning.* **❞**
>
> National Curriculum Task Group on Assessment and Testing, A Report, DES and the Welsh Office (HMSO, January 1988) V, para. 24

That might seem difficult enough, but due to timing they were required to do it without access to documentation regarding the National Curriculum subjects, what they might comprise and how they might be set out. Also, the task group could not predict how much, or as seems the case, how little liaison there would be between the different subject working groups.

They voiced some of the concerns that many educationalists and parents have about the idea of assessments and tests. Members of TGAT see the misgivings being based on fears that assessment will 'damage pupils', (ibid. III, para. 14); 'do damage to relationships between parents and schools', (ibid. III, para. 15); and that 'external tests will impose arbitrary restrictions on teachers' own work', (ibid. III, para. 16). They sense there is also concern that 'results will be published in league tables of scores, leading to ill-informed and unfair comparisons between schools', (ibid. III, para. 18). They do try to address each of these in turn, as follows.

Children   They see assessment and testing that is closely linked to the curriculum as enhancing motivation, giving children necessary short-term objectives, and pinpointing areas of learning need.

Parents and schools   They argue that national assessment criteria and calibration will give parents and children more understandable information, that is in relation to the general progress expected at an age, and not just by comparison with a class or year group in a particular school.

Teachers   Some teachers are concerned about formal assessments, because tests are often reductionist and focus on some small aspect of learning performance; tests restrict and interfere with the educative role of the teacher; and teachers also fear that tests erode their professional capacity to determine children's achievement and potential.

The TGAT attempt to allay these concerns is to say that the assessment procedures should be ones in which:

> **❝**   – *teachers' assessments over time and in normal learning contexts play an important part;*
> – *externally-provided methods and procedures are broad in scope and related to the curriculum attainment targets which all will share;*
> – *these assessment methods may often be incorporated into normal classroom activities;*
> – *the administration, marking and moderation procedures rely on the professional skills and mutual support of teachers, giving them both key responsibilities and communal safeguards against idiosyncrasy.* **❞**
>
> ibid. para. 16

If all these things happen with the implementation of the National Curriculum assessment arrangements, and you are given the necessary training and time to carry them out, the assessments will enhance your professional judgement.

Avoiding teaching to test

It is alarming that there is already in print a recommendation that teacher assessment should include some tasks which are like SATs, to use in years when the children will not be doing SATs. The suggestion is:

> 66 *that these tasks are undertaken about once a term.* 99
>
> DES and the Welsh Office, *Mathematics for Ages 5 to 16*. Proposals of the Secretary of State for Education and Science and the Secretary of State for Wales (HMSO, August 1988) 9.21, p. 81

We hope you will not find yourself 'teaching to test'. It is TGAT who commented that the assessment process:

> 66 *should be the servant, not the master, of the curriculum.* 99
>
> TGAT, A Report. Introduction, I, para. 4

There is less chance of teaching to test if many of the assessments can be made in the normal course of your work. In any case do not let the training and documentation force you to lose sight of your professional role. Teachers are educators. Your prime effort must be to enhance the teaching and learning for the children in your care. Teaching and learning are not about testing; but the assessment and testing that is now insisted upon can add to your insight into children's potential and progress during their years of schooling. Make it contribute rather than detract from the educative process.

To make a start on testing, it is necessary to check the jargon. Here are some key testing concepts put into the context of the National Curriculum.

Testing concepts explained

Criterion referencing

The first successful, wobbly, ride on a bicycle is part of the experience of most grown-ups. The criteria for success were measured in terms of making the pedals turn, hanging on, etc. The memory of passing the driving test brings similar things to mind, like whether you managed the indicators. These sorts of achievements can be, and are, measured against predetermined criteria. A criterion-referenced test is a test which allows individuals to measure themselves against external criteria. Master the criteria and you can pass the test. In other words, criterion referencing is tied to mastery learning, and ideally the learning should be such that when you take the test you pass.

Normal distribution

Whilst the National Curriculum offers the opportunity of judging children against criteria (attainment targets) the Education Reform Bill clearly offers the chance for comparison; child with child, class with class, and school with school. These comparisons will be made against the background of the statistical notion of normal distribution.

A normal distribution is what we call a graph of a particular shape. If we collect data about a large number of people and draw up a graph for each data item, some of the graphs will indicate that the proportions of people, with a particular score, are distributed so that the graph is a bell-shaped curve, as shown in Figure 9.1. Height, for example, and shoe size will provide that kind of graph, whereas what those people usually have for breakfast, or how many brothers they have would not.

The centre line on the graph in Figure 9.1 is the mean average. It is the average that we use in everyday talk. When individuals obtain scores away from the mean they are said to deviate from that mean. Whether or not the individual score is significantly distant from the mean is gauged in relation to the bands either side of the mean. The boundaries of those bands are called standard deviations. Two thirds of a class, on the basis of a smooth normal distribution curve, will lie within one standard deviation either side of the mean. Of the remaining third, who are reckoned to be significantly different, one sixth will be plus one standard deviation and one sixth minus one standard deviation. These proportions can be further broken down and in a class of, say, 30, only one child might be exceptionally different, in terms of, for example, mathematics skills, from the mean in either direction. But we all know about the classes which are better/worse than last year, or where there seems to be nobody in the middle ability range. A normal distribution curve is a model. Real classes, whilst offering a range of achievements, will not map straight onto a perfect bell shape.

Bandings like these are used to separate children in terms of their abilities, commonly their intellectual abilities. Children, and adults, are seen as being 'brighter', 'less able', 'gifted', having 'special needs', in relation to expectations which are based on the notion of a normal distribution.

There are two more averages that we can use in assessing children; the mode and the median. The mode is that average arrived at by seeing which score most children have obtained; it is the majority score. In relation to the National Curriculum we might see groups or classes being described as being at level 4 in, say, science. This is using the mode to describe what the majority have achieved.

The median is the score obtained by the child in the middle. To establish the median score place all the scores in rank order and the one halfway between the top and bottom is the median.

Subjectivity v. objectivity

The use of the word 'objective', in the context of assessment, implies the possibility of discovering the truth about an individual's achievement. To be objective is to suggest the absence of individual bias and, presumably, human fallibility. Clearly, absolute objectivity is unattainable.

Figure 9.1   A normal distribution curve

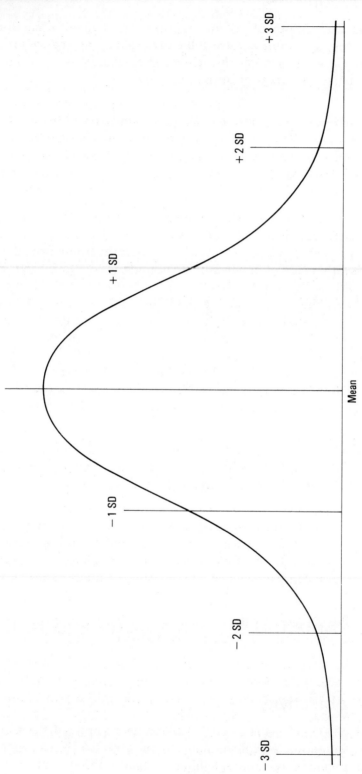

However, particularly in the formative assessment of individuals, we need to recognise and take account of our subjectivity to achieve balanced judgements. But we should not be afraid to see subjectivity as a strength rather than a weakness. Our expertise is built of more than a set of acquired skills; it is the way in which we assemble those skills and insights in order to form professional judgements. Published tests are often seen as being objective. By this is meant that they are value free and measures of discrete knowledge. However, these tests are actually the consequences of choice by the test constructor. The areas of knowledge to be tested are chosen, they do not present themselves. What is more important, both in published and teacher tests, is to guard against bias or prejudice. This kind of problem is not exclusively found in so-called subjective approaches, for it has to do with the suspension of critical appraisal in favour of predetermined interpretation.

Validity and reliability

Validity in assessment means that we assess what we say we will assess and the statement of intent is recognised as having usefulness in society. It is possible to assess most things. But valued and valuable assessment is valid assessment. It is perfectly possible to assess consistently, getting the same sort of pattern of results year after year, but still to be assessing the 'wrong things'. For example, it is possible to regularly give spelling lists and tests, which work reliably week in week out, but do not actually help children to learn to spell within their own writing. The spelling tests would be reliable but not valid in terms of the teaching of spelling! You can be a reliable assessor but your assessments may be invalid. If your assessments are valid they must be reliable!

Standardised tests

A standardised test is one that has been given to a national population sample at a specific age. The results in terms of spread of response are published, along with marking guidelines. SATs will be standardised, at least after the first full run, for national data will then be available to schools for comparison and moderation purposes.

Sources of information for assessment and testing

Information contributing to assessment of children's achievement can be drawn from a wide variety of sources. All are in teachers' ambit. We distinguish between those informal sources accessible to teachers in the normal course of their work, and formal external test outcomes, among which are SATs. Your own judgements of children's achievement, because they are wide-ranging and take place over time, are of far greater import than any batch of test scores. The weight of your assessment planning and implementation will be on the formative – 'what's the next step', rather than the summative – 'what step has been reached'.

Informal assessment

Teacher impressions, observations and judgements   In Chapter 8 we discussed the day-to-day observations of teachers undertaken during the normal processes of the classroom. The same arguments can be made in favour of giving credence to teacher's regular but informal reflections, in relation to fixed tasks. Do not discard what you learn about a child's achievement on the basis of it being informal and unstructured. Information gathered by you in your classroom may not be amenable to standardisation and generalisations but is very important. Methods of recording your impressions, such as diaries and audio recording, can now be part of your assessment repertoire.

You can supplement these observations with marks you give to assignments, written exercises and worksheets. In these cases you have already made an assessment or judgement about the standard of performance. The judgements can add to the qualitative observations.

Some kinds of performance are difficult to measure using external tests. It is on these that you can use your experience to systematise your observations. Performances that may be difficult to test include communication skills, problem-solving skills and physical skills. We will look at each of these skill sets in turn.

Teacher impressions: communication skills   The whole range of communication skills, that is, speaking, listening, dance, drama, creative writing, reading for meaning, etc. present test difficulties. For example, in reading, whilst the notion of reading age is convenient, it is important to appreciate that the National Curriculum is concerned as much, if not more, with the application of reading, rather than the obtaining of a particular reading age score. You need now, as has always been the case, to be aiming for reading for understanding, rather than reading for performance. You can do this better through structured observation of children's classroom learning than through the assembly of numbers of test scores.

Teacher impressions: problem solving   The production of novel and alternative solutions to problems is a creative act. It is difficult to imagine how such results might be regulated to fit into a formal, timetabled assessment schedule. It is feasible to set problems as formal assessment exercises, but the teacher's cumulative assessment of the child's ability to solve problems is of paramount importance. 'Eureka!' points have to be grasped in the here and now, and if the assessment task is a 'one off', the test day may not be the one on which children demonstrate their solving skills!

Teacher impressions: physical skills   There are two major, but related, sorts of physical ability we need to assess; performance in gross and fine physical activity. The former will often be identified in PE but will be amenable to assessment in other areas, for example, drama and dance. Fine control affects such skills as painting and handwriting, accuracy in measuring and drawing plans and maps. It is important to identify and assess skills across curriculum areas.

Pupil self-assessment   The National Curriculum subject working groups do document the importance of pupil self-assessment. The arguments for this are presented most cogently in the DES's *English for Ages 5 to 11:*

> **"** *Self-assessment by pupils themselves, even at the primary stage, has a part to play by encouraging a clear understanding of what is expected of them, motivation to reach it, a sense of pride in positive achievements, and a realistic appraisal of weakness that need to be tackled. It should be given due weight as part of the evidence towards the teacher's internal assessments.* **"**

7.19. p. 32

Formal assessment: tests

What children and teachers should know   In all tests children should be taught how to play the game. There are 'rules' to answering different sorts of test. For example, notes and single word answers may be appropriate in some situations, but would not do for a test of oracy or in an essay. However, in teaching children how to do tests we must distinguish between getting them to produce appropriate responses and the teaching of study skills which will be of continuing value through formal education and beyond. We can teach children how to study, and how to tackle assessment demands. There is little point in teaching children just to 'pass'. On the whole tests are contrived and unlike real life. Skill in doing tests may not help in coping with real problems.

Teachers are all accustomed to pencil and paper tests. Before we give a test, though, we should check that it is appropriate and understand its strengths and weaknesses. Here are a number of kinds of written test explained.

Multiple choice   These are tests where a range of alternative answers are offered to a given question. Children have to select the correct answer. Multiple-choice tests are easy to mark but not so easy to construct. If you are going to use them, it is important to construct your question very clearly and in a way which does not point to a particular answer. Whilst multiple-choice tests do allow you to cover a lot of content, children are being tested more on recall and specific question comprehension than on overall understanding. Multiple-choice items are often used in verbal reasoning tests.

Yes–no   This is the one-right-answer type of test. The most common approach is for teacher to read out questions and for the children to write down their answers. The popularity of these sorts of test is rooted in teacher security, ease of operation and ease of marking. However, they have many drawbacks. There is no opportunity to give sophisticated responses and creative answers, no matter how 'right'. There are plenty of examples of wrong answers which actually were correct responses to other interpretations of the question.

Essays   Essay writing is often associated with 'creative writing'. In school children write many more factual than imaginative pieces. The emphasis on testing extended writing through the stimulus of a fictional format is therefore potentially distorting. If you wish to use or set essays as a means of assessing children's writing, do make sure you offer a range of opportunities which reflect the available range of writing purposes. Essays do allow the children's development of an idea, and their planning, organisation and concentration to be assessed. The disadvantage is to do with the quality of work to be read and marked, and the criteria against which answers will be judged. The logistical problems are clear enough. The problems with regard to criteria are more complex. The judging of a piece of prose or non-fiction is affected by such considerations as style, length, values and legibility. Despite adopting marking strategies such as five marks for this, three marks for that and so on, the judgement of the teacher will emerge as the major determining factor. What may help is the development, under the National Curriculum, of moderation systems.

Comprehension   There are two main sorts of comprehension exercises in common use in classrooms: sentence provision and sentence completion. In the former children are commonly presented with a passage and a set of questions on that passage. They respond by writing sentences. Sometimes the sentences are provided in a multiple-choice approach but the principles remain the same. What is being tested is the child's ability to interpret the passage. The other main approach is to offer part answers which the child has to complete. This can be in relation to a passage, or free-standing sentences. What is being tested here is not only understanding, but also the ability of children to select appropriate vocabulary, and the correct grammar. In other words the activity has dimensions other than those traditionally associated with comprehension exercises.

The advantages of sentence provision exercises are that they are easy to set and mark. But they can be repetitive and tedious, particularly when the passages are interesting but incomplete! Sentence completion offers an often stimulating puzzle to children, but that is its weakness – what is really being assessed?

Cloze procedure is an extension of sentence completion. Here a passage is offered in which words are left out at predetermined intervals. Commonly every fifth or seventh word is omitted. Children have to fill in the missing word, either the exact word or sometimes a suitable alternative. Cloze procedure offers you a range of diagnostic opportunities. In this respect it is not only an extension of the sentence completion activities but also a very good way of getting to grips with, for example, vocabulary, logic, grammar and sentence construction. These are the strengths of cloze, but it does take time to prepare and respond to, and you need to make time to work with small groups and individuals.

SATs: a new broad test

The members of TGAT recognise that four criteria are especially important in national assessment. The assessments should be:

> **"** *criterion-referenced*
> *formative*
> *moderated*
> *related to progression.* **"**

TGAT, A Report, I, para. 5

With these criteria in mind they have conceived of SATs as being rather more than what is commonly thought of as a test.

SATs will vary according to three aspects or modes.

The presentation mode is about how the questions are given to the children (whether orally, written, pictorially, on the video or computer, or by practical demonstration).

The operation mode is how the children will work on the problem (whether exclusively mentally, through writing, practically or orally).

The response mode is how the children will answer. For example, this could be by choosing a written answer from a range of possibilities, by writing an answer, by answering orally, by working practically while the teacher observes, by making something, by making something happen, or by generating a computer input.

It seems likely that schools will be provided with a dossier of possible choices regarding assessment, and that teachers will select, from these, tasks which present various combinations of the modes of presentation, operation and response.

The working groups did offer some advice to the agencies devising SATs. For example, in science:

> *The banks of tasks should be wide-ranging so that teachers have a great deal of choice in selecting material which is likely to be of particular value and relevance to their pupils and to the context in which the learning activities have taken place. They should be imaginative, interesting to pupils and stretching.*
>
> DES and the Welsh Office, *Science for Ages 5 to 16.* Proposals of the Secretary of State for Education and Science and the Secretary of State for Wales (HMSO, August 1988) 6.39. p. 90

For English the following advice appears:

> *... assessment should pay attention to the process as well as the product of the task: to the way in which children approach and sustain it, the elements in which they have particular difficulties or strengths as well as the quality of the finished work; ...*
>
> *English for Ages 5 to 11,* 7.11, p. 31

No sample SATs are available yet, but the TGAT report does give an example of the type of task which 'will serve to illustrate how carefully structured class activities could provide opportunities for systematic assessment, in a range of profile components within a context of activity that was meaningful and motivating for a primary pupil'. This is the example they give:

"A task for seven-year-olds

The following task was one of several used with an infant class of 5–7 year old children as part of a topic entitled 'winter through to spring'. The task involved estimation, observation, measuring, drawing sensible conclusions and recording, and there were opportunities at various points throughout for the assessment of profiles in language (oral and written), mathematics and science (problem-solving and measurement). The children, in the main, worked in groups and arrived at conclusions collaboratively although there was ample opportunity for individual work.

First activity – discussion, interviewing, collecting data

Language *Question asked: How do we keep warm in winter?*
Discussion.

Maths *Make a survey of the clothes worn by the children in the classroom.*

Maths/art *Record this information (graph).*

Second activity – estimation, measurement of temperature and time

Language *Question asked: Which materials keep us warmest?*
Wrap one layer of a different material around each of six milk bottles – cotton, fur, wool, felt, newspaper, nylon.

Science *Fill the bottles with warm water.*

And maths *Measure the temperature in each, using a thermometer, and record it.*
Estimate which bottle of water will cool first.
Measure the temperature every half-hour and record.
Which bottle of water grows cold first?
Why?
Which stayed warm?
Why?

Third activity – estimation, measurement of temperature and time, problem solving, recording, discussion, sequencing, writing, computer work

Science *Question asked: What would help to keep the bottles of water warm longer?*

Language *Discussion*

Science *Repeat the experiment, first wrapping four layers of one type of material around each bottle.*
Are the results different?
How?
Why?
Which material kept the water warm longest?

Maths *Put the materials into sequence, coolest to warmest.*

Health education *How is it best to dress in cold weather?*

Language *Write, or use the computer to write, the story of this experiment.* **"**

TGAT, A Report, Appendix D

In principle it seems to us that SATs are going to incorporate many aspects similar to those found in topic work.

- ▶ There will be a variety of tasks, given in a range of ways and allowing different ways of responding.

- ▶ The children will be assessed on more than one aspect of learning during an activity.

- ▶ There will be practical components in what they do.

- ▶ There will be opportunities for group work and for individual work.

- ▶ There will be some degree of flexibility and possibly open-endedness about the tasks.

- ▶ Elements of the task will be novel.

A positive spin-off from the introduction of national assessments may be an increase in primary school topic work. If you want the children in your class to try the kind of task that may feature in an SAT, choose some part of one of the topics planned for them. Work out the specific problems and tasks in detail, to cover that aspect of the topic. Decide how the problems are to be presented, worked on and recorded. Then structure the work groups appropriately. Arrange a timetable for yourself and the rest of the class (there are hints on this in Chapter 4); put it into action, for a few children at a time, when you can give them your attention. Make judgements about the level of each child's performance against what they were asked to do. Clearly, this kind of assignment cannot be given to children 'cold'. You could not expect children who were unused to group work, practical work without you, or problem-solving to know where to start. The children will need to tackle some other topics, using these aspects first. The key is to plan ahead so that you and they can then 'have a go'. It will alert you to some of the management problems of external assessment.

Interpretation of assessment information

The interpretation of assessment outcomes is a vital but fraught activity. Interpretations can easily drift from being rational deductions and diagnosis based on the data to hand, to become stereotypical or idealised conclusions. To guard against inappropriate interpretations, it is necessary to bear the following ideas in mind:

- ▶ The fact that normal distribution is a model.

- ▶ The validity and reliability of the type of assessment.

- ▶ External influences on the test situation and the child.

- ▶ Learning is longitudinal and formal assessment only a snapshot.

- ▶ All areas of learning are related and interdependent and assessments are therefore 'unreal'.

- ▶ The danger of your imposing your prior expectations on the data.

The compilation and interpretation of SATs results will also bring problems. Once the test tasks have been constructed and during trialling, instructions will be set out regarding the weighting of results to compile an overall result, for a profile component. This issue is, at the time of writing, under consideration by SEAC.

For whole-school reporting, SAT results will be aggregated. We should remember that results have the most meaning for the individual child if the tasks are criterion referenced. Aggregation is really problematic not least because all children's results when combined will 'average' out and bring them closer to the mean average for the class. This can lead to situations where attempts are made to rank children using results which appear to have very small differences between them. We believe that the use of profiling and records of achievement will be the response to aggregation problems.

If we speculate about SAT tasks, for example, as a part of a SAT taking in English AT1, children may be required to engage in a small group discussion of how to tackle a problem. The teacher observes, and notes the following for each child:

Level 1	takes part	listens speaks
Level 2	focus on task	listens to what others say about task speaks about task
Level 3	focus on task	listens to others' suggestions throughout makes suggestions asks questions/comments on what others say answers questions/further develops contribution in reply.

The teacher records at which level each child operates. When all the class have done the task, she counts the number of children operating at each level for this profile component (English PC1). This will give the class 'scores' (perhaps something like 5 level 1, 18 level 2, 7 level 3). These will contribute to the class assessments and will be scrutinised at moderation meetings.

Tests and equal opportunities

Boys and girls perform differently in tests. Performance differences are partly attributable to the milieu in which the test is given, what is in the test, and the layout of the questions.

> **“** *The multiple choice format appears to favour boys as does practical testing.* **”**
>
> TGAT, A Report, Appendix F 3.5.

In test construction the problem of bias regarding gender and race has been raised by TGAT. They recommend that SATs are regularly reviewed to guard against the presence of such biases. Where a child's first language is not English, it has been suggested that assessment, where possible and appropriate, be conducted in the child's own first language.

It seems possible that sex distribution and racial composition may add to the vaguely mentioned socio-economic factors which LEAs are asked to address in the whole-school reports.

With regard to children with special needs, those who are able to enter the national assessment tests should be encouraged to do so. Special tests will also be devised for those children for whom the national SATs are inappropriate.

Moderation

In order that assessments have meaning beyond the child, class or school, the judgements of individual teachers need to be compared with others, and a shared understanding about standards needs to be reached. Moderation is familiar to teachers working with GCSE, and in further and higher education, but has never been part of the culture of the primary school. It is not the same as inspection.

We are partly making predictions now, but it seems likely that, at the end of the school year, teachers of pupils at key stages (top infant and top junior teachers) will attend meetings involving a group of schools. To the meetings they will take a sample of their own continuous assessment records (pupils profiles etc.), a summary achievement sheet for all the children in their class, samples of children's work, and results of the SATs the children have done. At the meeting, all these will be compared with those of the other teachers present, and with countrywide national assessments. Any discrepancies will be discussed by the group and it will be decided whether they are due to the teachers' own criteria used for making judgements, local factors within the schools and their contexts, or something awry with SATs nationally. An agreed distribution of results will be collectively decided upon for each school.

Moderation is a serious business. The role of moderator is one that demands sensitivity, diplomacy and professionalism. Moderators have to be able to make judgements, back them up and present their views in a balanced but determined way. Moderation requires the collaboration of all those involved. Typically moderators will expect to sample work from your school with guidance but not under control, and will have the power to reduce, or raise, your estimates of children's achievements.

As it seems that moderation will be a group activity, where all the teachers share the task, the burden of responsibility as well as the fear of being moderated will be common to and understood by everyone. However, it is important to be clear that, although schools will share moderators and they may be colleagues well known to you, this will not affect the elements of control implicit in the moderation role. On the positive side moderation is a good way of passing on good practice, and, once the initial shock is over, is a reassuring way of confirming professional standards.

Assessment of teachers

All that we have said relates to judgements being made about the performance of children. Teacher appraisal will also be a feature of the education system of the 1990s. Teachers will feel under scrutiny when key stage and school performance reports are made available. There will also be regular self-development and career review discussions. Teacher assessment is formative, not summative!

Summary

Key stage 1 assessment

Timing of implementation of reports on assessment   The first reported assessments at key stage 1, in English, mathematics and science, will be in 1992. There will be an unreported assessment in the preceding year.

Tasks for teachers   The TGAT Report makes it clear that the pattern of assessment will fit in with their recommendations, if teachers perform a number of specific tasks in the year when children have their seventh birthday (typically this will be in the top infants). These tasks are as follows:

1   Using their own continuous assessment records of what has been taught and learned, to apply their professional judgement to say what levels each child in their care has reached, across a number of profile components.
2   To choose three SATs from a national bank, at least one of these being the same as that chosen by other schools in the area.
3   Using standard ways of setting the tasks and writing down the children's performance, to put the test tasks into their teaching and learning programme, so that each child is assessed on performance in three tasks across the profile components.
4   To go to a local group moderation meeting to consider, discuss and agree a common standard concerning the range and distribution of test results.
5   To write a report on the children's overall performance compared with local and national results, for the headteacher, the governors and the LEA to read.
6   To report on each child's achievements to their parents.
7   To place the results in school records.

Key stage 2 assessment

This will not take effect until well into the 1990s, so there is room for new initiatives. However, at present, the recommendations are that, for children at age 11, the same tasks will be carried out by teachers, as for children at age 7. There will be some additions, as follows:

1   To administer other additional tests.
2   To make a statement of school performance publicly, within a report which mentions the school's context.
3   To make the children's test performance scores available, in confidence, to the secondary school to which they go on.

CHAPTER 10
RECORD KEEPING

Why schools need records

There is an idea shared by many people in education, that writing things down seals them in the past, and makes them of little future use. Teaching and learning are about process and dynamism, but good internal records can fuel the dynamic and sense of teamwork within a school.

The introduction of the National Curriculum highlights the importance of continuity and progression within and across schools. In some ways it will become easier for you to compile consistent internal records of teaching and learning, for you can begin to use items from the National Curriculum documents as headings. However, there are many other things that will need recording as well.

It seems likely that standard summative forms will be produced locally and nationally, and that teachers will be pressed into completing these. We shall therefore focus on ways of setting down continuous assessments in class, and 'hand-on' forms within a school. We shall also look at whole school records. All these within-school records can reflect the teacher's and school's own ethos, and are more flexible and open to change.

What is put on record?

All that teachers do has a record attached to it. How many on roll? How many present? How many in this group or that? Where's a child 'up to'? What has a group achieved this session? What did Jon do yesterday afternoon? What are group X going to be doing on Friday afternoon?

Teacher records   Teacher records are about teaching. They are often personal and idiosyncratic and need to be tied in with planning. For example a tick list saying which groups have done pond dipping with you, and whose turn it is to do it and discuss their findings next, is an example of a teacher record. Teacher records are cumulative. They may also be summative, in that when a planned programme of work is completed, in teaching terms, the record can be set aside. When a planned topic has been worked through and you are ready to move on to the next, all your written work attached to the topic can be put away, for later reference.

Child records   Child records are about learning; that is, learning completed and the learning that, according to the teacher's planning, will happen next.

Records of both teaching and learning can be of two kinds: past and future. We can represent these kinds of records, for both teacher and child, as shown in Figure 10.1.

Figure 10.1   Kinds of records for teaching and learning

	TEACHER	CHILD
PAST	**TICK LISTS (Review)** Topics completed Elements of programmes of study worked on	**PORTFOLIO (Achievements)** Levels reached Test results Work samples
FUTURE	**PLANS (Forecast)** Overview Lesson plans	**PROFILE (Potential)** Next steps for learning

Records of the past

Records to do with the past are of achievements and completions. For example, Mundip can conserve to 10; Julia has read a range of books at that level; I have developed a way of teaching the concept of time which works. These are often easy to record, and whether or not there's a tick on a form or list, we have a mental tick system. 'Ah, that's that done!'. Test results commonly fit this pattern.

Teacher records: past (what has been taught?)

Teacher records can include the following:

> Ticking a list against children's names (concepts taught and to whom)
> Details of subject teaching across term or year
> Details of across curriculum studies, for example topic work
> Past lesson plans and outcomes
> Class logs.

All of these, in one form or another, will be familiar to you, apart from perhaps, the use of class logs. It is possible to use the notion of a log in the classroom. As the school log records the travels of a school over generations, so can a class log record the voyages of children and their teacher over a few weeks, a term or a year. The purpose of logs is to enable you to transmit the flavour of your classroom over time. It should be a document which anyone could read and thereby gain some insights into your working world. Where the log differs from a diary is in the nature of the information recorded and the format for recording. Try keeping a log for half a term. You should write your log every day, certainly every week, and record: major events, changes in routines, changes in direction, illnesses that affect many children, important conversations with children, teachers, parents or others.

All of these notes should be kept in date order. The pay-off for your class is twofold; you will gain reassurance about development, and you will find that your reading of the log will help sensitise you to issues for closer investigation.

Child records: past (what are his/her achievements, problems?)

Child records may include:

> Samples of work done
> Test results
> Levels reached in National Curriculum attainment targets
> Health/life experiences
> Social competences
> Child's own 'work done' record
> Outcomes of parent consultations.

Whole-school: past (what has happened?)

Examples of whole school records are:

> School log books
> School events
> Letters file
> Resources acquired
> Changes in roll and staffing.

Records of the future

While it is important for children (and their parents) to know 'where they have got to' and vital for the teacher and new school to know what has been completed and achieved, it is even more important to have a view of what happens next. Teachers needs a vision of potential progress and process, not only for each child they teach, but also about every aspect of their own teaching.

Records relating to the future draw as much from 'error', failure and lack of understanding as they do from past success. This applies to the teacher's teaching just as it does to the children's learning. If all the children in a group continue to need teacher support after a concept has been taught them, it is a sign that teaching was incomplete and should be tackled again, more fully or in different ways. If Celia consistently gets subtraction sums wrong or cannot write sentences without help, records should indicate action for understanding. Action may mean more practice, but not without teacher intervention and monitoring.

Teacher records: future (what is planned?)

Ways of planning future teaching are:

> Term plan of the whole curriculum
> Term plan of the National Curriculum
> Term plan of the core curriculum
> Term plan of across-curriculum activities
> One week's lesson plans
> Priority plans for groups or individual children.

Child records: future (what are the next steps for learning?)

Ways of recording a child's progress with a view to the future are:

> Current health problems
> Special needs
> Curriculum areas for potential growth (has achieved past success)
> Curriculum areas for remediation (little or no progression in evidence, or systematic error record)
> Social development profile – for example, needs to be given more responsibility, to organise his/her own resources.

Whole-school records: future (school development plans)

When it comes to the whole school you might take note of:

> Curriculum areas for maintenance
> Curriculum areas for remediation
> In-service needs
> Development profile – for example, co-ordination and resource responsibilities
> Whole curriculum plan
> Phased plan for National Curriculum implementation
> School plan of across-curriculum activities
> Periodic review of administrative structures and roles
> Decisions taken.

What records should look like

Content and layout

No teacher wants to be snowed under by charts, tables and checklists. They inhibit your involvement in the children's learning, the children's access to you and can stifle your own learning. Written records need to be devised that are quick to do, succinct but meaningful and complete. They also need to fit a clipboard, or the desk corner.

A tick is brief but it doesn't tell you much. A tick says 'done it', but does it mean: done it well; done it better; written without errors; read with expression; read with few mistakes; or could do more? A tick is too brief, unless it is of the variety that adds to your notes and your memory.

You can make a tick list a bit more sensitive as a recording device by, for example, a dot for 'started' and a tick over for 'finished', or two ticks to record this. A triangle is also a good idea because it is clear (see Figure 10.2). This could refer to a statement of attainment.

For 'hand-on' purposes within a school, if you record learning in, for example, mathematics, in terms of programme of study points taught to which children, statements of attainment in which attainment targets worked on and levels worked at and mastered by each child, you will probably provide the next teachers with the minimum they need to know about the past mathematical experience and development of the children you have taught.

Figure 10.2   Record keeping: an alternative to a tick (√)

The record goes like this:

concept introduced　　　　　　/　　　　　concept worked on　　　　⌊　　　　　concept mastered　　　　△

It may be argued that teachers do not want to know what has been taught, only what has been learned. For evaluation and teamwork purposes it may be important to record teaching too. The form your record takes may reflect whether you have taught much or little through topics, and how you have tackled subject teaching (see Section B). The whole school may devise a standard form, so that your own notes can be entered, however you have approached your teaching.

Some suggested record layouts are shown in Figures 10.3, 10.4 and 10.5.

Figure 10.3   Mathematics child record: level 1

MATHEMATICS CHILD RECORD: level 1 NAME:　　　　　　　CLASS(ES):		INTRODUCED	WORKED ON	MASTERED	TEACHER'S COMMENTS
PC1 AT: 1	(Number/measures) Use materials Talk/ask questions Predict				
2	Numbers to 10 Conserve				
3	+ − to 10				
4	Estimate to 10				
5	Repeat patterns				
8	Compare/order objects (pre-measure)				
PC2 AT: 9	(Shape/space/problems) Use materials Talk/ask questions Predict				
10	Sort 2D/3D shapes Build/draw/describe shapes				
11	Position vocabulary Understand linear movement				
12	Sorting				
13	Practical recording Mapping				
14	Understand idea of probability				

Figure 10.4 Mathematics: teacher's record sheet, AT3 level 1

N.B. The statements of attainment have been teased out to indicate steps for mastery.

MATHEMATICS AT3 level 1							TEACHER'S RECORD SHEET
Name of child	Addition without recording to 10	Addition with some recording to 10	Subtraction without recording to 10	Subtraction with some recording to 10	Formal addition to 10	Formal subtraction to 10	Teacher's comments

Audience

The type of record chosen will depend on the audience it is for. However, we cannot always predict who will read or require information in a record. It is unwise to have a full but unorthodox exchange of information between yourself and the one other teacher who will be in charge of your class next year. You or that teacher may find yourselves taking a different class or job. The records may be required by the headteacher or educational psychologist.

What to do with records you receive

Reading and interpreting them

The first thing to do with records is to read them! This may sound obvious but it does not always happen. Many teachers work in primary schools with elaborate internal record systems, where some staff members simply pay no regard to what any teacher before them has said about the past performance or potential of children now in their care.

After a summer break, children must not be asked to start again on a programme of work that they have done already. Some teachers have insisted on this in the past, their reasoning being that, firstly it is good revision, and secondly, the children had probably forgotten it in the summer anyway. Do not make children repeat work, unless there are strong indications, for each individual, that they need to do so. There is too much to do to effectively waste children's time

Figure 10.5 Mathematics PC1: child record

MATHEMATICS PC1 SUMMARY SHEET NAME: CLASSES:

AT	LEVEL 1	DATE MASTERED	AT	LEVEL 2	DATE MASTERED	AT	LEVEL 3	DATE MASTERED
1	Use materials Talk/ask questions Predict		1	Choose appropriate maths/materials Describe work/record Check Hypothesise		1	Choose appropriate maths/materials Check results Explain work/record systematically Make and test predictions	
2	Numbers to 10 Conserve		2	Numbers to 100 Place value ½ ¼		2	Numbers to 1000 Decimal notation with money Negative whole numbers	
3	+ − to 10		3	+ − to 10 Difference + − problems		3	+ − to 20 × ÷ problems × to 5 × 5, 2, 5, 10× tables	
4	Estimate to 10		4	Estimate to 20		4	Approximation Remainders	
5	Repeat patterns		5	+ − patterns to 10 Odd and even		5	Explain number patterns Find/use number patterns in mental work Whole numbers ÷ by 2, 5, 10	
8	Compare/order objects (pre-measure)		6	Symbol for unknown number		6	Input/output from machines	
			8	Non-standard measures Coins Common units of length/capacity/'weight'/time		8	Use metric units Choose/use appropriate units Estimate	

123

with unnecessary repetition. The National Curriculum is only the statutory minimum that must be done! If the children have the time, they can always do more!

Some teachers of new classes have often set records aside until they feel they have formed their own first impressions of their pupils. The thinking behind this is to reduce the chance that the pupils' past performance may colour the present teacher's thinking and expectations. There is the idea that these expectations may become self-fulfilling. It does represent a justified concern about the subjectivity of the teacher. However, teacher subjectivity is there, whether you read records sooner or later. First impressions are just as suspect as any others. Most importantly, past performance, and this includes behavioural and attitudinal elements, must be the starting point for future planning.

A school internal record is pointless unless somebody acts on it, and that does not mean just handing it on! The expectations you have of your colleagues, that they will read and act on what you record, must be in line with what you yourself do for records you receive.

The primary school's reception teacher has no such record bank to act on. Her record resource is oral and comes from the parents. Health problems and illness, orientation to school, attitudes to learning, support in the home and support of links with school are all part of that information she must draw on. It will be tempting for schools to test children on entry, when SATs are in full use and 'results' are public. We would urge caution. There is no point in producing data about very young children, which may indicate the success or failure of parenting! It would be more profitable to regard the early years as being about enabling not labelling.

Keeping records safe

Look after records that come into your care. You need to put them in a safe locked place to which only named people have a key. You must do this because they are confidential and it would betray the trust parents and children place in you if records were accessible to unauthorised people; also because they often represent the accumulation of much work done by several teachers, and are therefore irreplaceable. Remember that records are still confidential when you can recall what is in them. Be discreet or your professionalism is undermined.

Reports

To parents   Reports to parents will comprise a list of levels reached in the profile components for each core subject, in combination with the results of the SATs completed by the child. Similar lists will be added for the other foundation subjects when these programmes of study and attainment targets have been produced and introduced into schools. In the meantime, reporting may be confined to the core subjects, with the classteacher commenting on other learning orally, in a consultation with each child's parents. In due course, but this may be a long while ahead for some children in primary schools, a profile will be completed for each child, to include a record of achievement and other aspects of development.

Within school   Teachers decide how profile component data can be combined to give the basis for an internal review.

Whole-school performance   These reports will be made publicly available, and will be compiled by each school, and ratified by the LEA. The results will not be adjusted in relation to the school catchment area etc. but the LEA will be able to set down factors which they feel may affect the results obtained by schools in the area. Schools are not required to publish the results obtained by seven-year-olds to a wider audience than parents, governors and providers, but they may choose to do so.

Summary

Records grow out of practice and expectation; they are not self-justifying. This means that the form and nature of internal school records must reflect the curriculum decisions taken within the school. However, in communicating across schools and within LEAs there will be a level of conformity of practice. This will need to come out of moderation activity. In the first instance, however, records are likely to be adaptations of existing practices.

Clift and his colleagues made the following general recommendations about records.

> **"** *The formulation of records should always be a collaborative exercise involving all the teachers within a primary school.* **"**

> **"** *When records are also intended to communicate information to the next stage in education, the scope of the collaboration should extend to the recipients.* **"**

> **"** *. . . if record keeping is to be rather more than an end of day or weekly activity, and seen as part of the process of teaching, then teachers need to be freed of many of the non-teaching and supervisory activities commonly a part of primary school life.* **"**
>
> Clift, P. et al, *Record Keeping in Primary Schools* (Macmillan, 1981)

The National Curriculum requirements do not invalidate these conclusions. If anything they strengthen them, for detailed and consistent records are essential for continuity and progression.

In compiling your in-school records it is important to:

> ▶   consult and develop them collaboratively

> ▶   ensure that records are about the future as well as the past

> ▶   interpret records widely and not give higher status to records which carry marks

> ▶   have records which permit individual progress to be identified and not masked through aggregation.

The future of records is most likely to be in the development of profiling.

DEVELOPING ACTION PLANS

This section is about the priorities you may choose to adopt in introducing the National Curriculum to your classroom and school. Suggestions are made as to how you may take action for change. The purposes are to give support in:

▶ identifying central elements of good practice

▶ collecting information on current practice

▶ developing your action plan for change and development.

Introduction

In deciding what will be most helpful to you, in terms of action now, we have avoided handy hints about programmes of study and attainment targets. After all the minimum content of the core curriculum is now set, and most of the rest will be available in writing soon.

We have deliberately left out discussion of the merits of this or any particular curriculum. We just want to help you make the best of it, and view it as leading to increased teacher professionalism and competence and thorough broad-based learning opportunities for children and teachers alike.

How you devise ways of teaching particular children this or that is an area in which you are already the expert. Much of what we have said in Section B will support you. What we are doing here is focusing on the most important areas which make a difference to the whole curriculum delivery of any teacher.

Focusing on the important issues

There are too many things happening in schools and classrooms for us to grapple with them all at the same time. The range of information available to us is far greater than we can cope with. This is the case in all complex human activity. It is necessary to make choices and to prioritise. In organising your thoughts to create an agenda for action based upon balanced judgements it is helpful to have manageable parcels of information. The descriptions and suggested activities which follow are constructed in order to help you sift through the great amount of information which surrounds the teacher.

Good delivery supported by clear planning and organisation is a sign of good practice and is independent of the vagaries of content. The National Curriculum will not pose major problems for you if you have good planning, good use of time, good communication and so on. So, in this section we are focusing on those areas of classroom practice and school organisation which we see as underpinning all of the things which you need to examine in your delivery of the whole curriculum.

Action

Action can only be effective if you know where you are starting from. Many of the things we do have been developed through intuition and tradition. We all know how fascinating it is to visit other schools and see how things are done there. It is most revealing when we find common problems being tackled in quite different ways. This can be a real eye-opener and lead to questions like, 'Why didn't we think of that?' The answer is not about our abilities but about our expectations and perspectives. These are often framed by the particular ethos in which we are working. Being more objective about your classroom and school can bring about a reappraisal of what you are doing now. In all of the areas we have identified we are adopting the principle that before you can change things you must be absolutely clear about your current practice. You are then well placed to make changes in directions over which you can have proper control. The actions you take on the basis of analysis are likely to be more fruitful than those taken on the basis of intuition. But do take action progressively, one step at a time.

Whilst the content framework in which you are working is prescribed by the National Curriculum, it is the case that you are responsible for its effective delivery. To enhance your effectiveness it is necessary to develop your own action plan. This plan must be enabling and empowering to you, your colleagues and the children in your care.

How to use this section

The whole of the book will support you in getting to grips with the National Curriculum in action. This section will help you to determine your own priorities and action agenda. The emphasis in here is on classteachers. The approach we would invite heads to take is to use Chapter 11 to clarify where your teachers are, and as a means to identify such things as in-service needs. Similar issues are further developed in Chapter 12 and additional whole-school considerations are raised there.

CHAPTER

11

CLASSTEACHERS

Before you can take action, you need to reflect on the kind of teacher you are now. You can then be more realistic about your strengths and weaknesses when implementing change. Match yourself against the following two contrasting models.

Teaching style

Teacher A

If you feel more confident and successful teaching the whole class for much of the time, with your own timetable (that is, teacher time) setting the pace, some of your strengths, upon which you can build, are these:

▶ Your planning is logical and linear and your aims are clear.

▶ Timing is slick because you are in control of both your own and the children's to a high degree.

▶ Most talk involves you 'in the chair' so you can monitor and influence the outcomes of lines of argument.

▶ The possible areas for evaluation are clear; they have to do with your own performance and the outcomes of the children's learning.

The points which need looking at are:

▶ Are your plans too narrow, do they take account of each child, and can the children have learning experiences in school, other than with you?

▶ Is the timing elastic enough to allow serendipity, novel approaches and finishing off?

▶ Are there enough opportunities for children to exchange ideas and learn from each other?

▶ Are there opportunities for children to develop a line of thinking or working without our intervention?

▶ Does everyone get a chance to contribute to the running of the class and the teaching and learning processes?

▶ Are there opportunities for pupil self-appraisal and can the children sometimes be the agents of change?

Teacher B

If your approach is to set up individual work programmes for each child in your care, then the strengths you can build on are these:

▶ Your plans are detailed and the match between child and task is high.

▶ Timing for each learning task is elastic; the child sets the pace.

▶ Your teaching dialogue, questions and questioning, is on a one-to-one basis and can fit the needs of the child; no child is overlooked.

▶ Evaluations can start with each individual child.

The areas which need monitoring are as follows:

▶ Is there a continuity of learning which matches the school ethos and gives a sense of community, amongst the children and with colleagues?

▶ Are you using your time effectively, or are you finding there is repetition of teaching as each child reaches another point in their conceptual development?

▶ Do children have the opportunity to learn mutual support, co-operation and teamwork?

▶ Is there a chance for children's own ideas to fire each other's learning?

▶ Can you undertake whole class evaluations to alter the classroom processes?

You probably find you are somewhere between these two approaches. Whatever your favoured style of organisation, some of the points mentioned above will be those to bear in mind when working through the rest of this chapter.

Priorities for the classteacher

For the classteacher there are five main areas of concern. In each of these areas we make suggestions for ways of finding out where you are now. Then you can decide where change is a good idea and can choose ways of setting about it. In other words it is about improving your efficiency and effectiveness, 'smartening up your act' and staying 'on top'. The areas are these:

Planning
Time management
Groups and grouping
Questions and questioning
Evaluation and assessment.

Planning

Current planning

Planning takes place at levels which are dependent on the time needed for implementation. So:

Short term plan: One week
Medium term plan: One school term
Long term plan: One or more school years.

Exercise   List the sorts of plans you make under three headings:

Academic work
Administration
School requirements e.g. assemblies, special events.

To what extent do these plans offer short, medium and/or long term opportunities?

Questions

What sort of plans do you make for a week?
What does the school expect?
How do your term plans relate to your weekly plans?
What level of planning do you do for the year?
Which of these plans do you make simply for other people, which actually are of no use to you?
What plans do you make for yourself that are also really of no use to you?
What plans do you make for the children that are no use to them, and how do you know?

Action to change your planning

Changing plans you make for others   Negotiate to change the form of the plans which you make for other staff to see, in a way that will be useful to you too. Do this by:

▶ writing down what the plan needs to show for your use

▶ finding out and writing down what the plan needs to show for other people to use it

▶ compiling a combined content list

▶ devising a layout which presents the content clearly.

Changing plans you make for yourself   If you are inappropriately planning for yourself, change your strategy by:

▶ writing down what the plan needs to show

▶ devising a layout which presents the content clearly.

Changing plans you make for the children   Make plans for the children that work by:

▶ discussing with them what they need on the plan

▶ showing them the proposed layout and making sure it is clear to them

▶ getting them to appraise where outcomes did not match plans.

The better your planning, the better you will be able to handle whatever prescriptions the National Curriculum brings.

Time management

Current time management

Exercise   Where does your time go? Find out using Chapter 6.

The amount of time that children spend on their work varies considerably from school to school and class to class. Research indicates that the longer children have on task the more progress they make. It is important, therefore, to gauge the amount of time your children have to do their work and to see whether you can improve on this.

Exercise   Keep a log of the times that sessions actually start and finish. Do this for a week. Include times when the children are being taught as a whole class. Exclude times when children are being given information about such things as dinner arrangements, sports days and so on. Exclude one-off occasions, e.g. the visitor who talks about an event, a cause and so on unless this is part of a planned programme of work. How many hours a week do your class get to attend to their work? Is this enough in your view for them to achieve what they need to achieve?

Time on task is sometimes limited by children's behaviour. You will know which children disrupt their own or other's work. (There's an example worked through in Chapter 8.)

Exercise   Observe one of the children you are concerned about.
Keep a daily diary.
Set up a case conference.

Exercise   Make a list of your classroom rules and any school rules that you are required to uphold in your classroom. Keep a check for one week on the frequency with which you have to remind children of the rules. List those rules which mean the children have to get permission in order to carry out the next stage of their particular task.

Questions

What happens at the beginnings and ends of sessions?

Are there spaces in the timetable?

What sort of timetable do you prefer: everything timetabled; some things timetabled; or nothing apart from rooms timetabled?

What do you do when children finish quickly? Do you provide additional learning activities?

What do you do when they take longer than you expect? Do you provide enough time for everyone to finish, at least on some occasions?

What do you do when a task runs across breaks or goes on from one day to the next? Can the children press their own learning as far as possible, before being asked to abandon it in favour of something else?

Are there any rules which seem to be interrupting children's time on task? What classroom rules need changing?

Action to change time management

Changing the use of teacher's time   When you know where you can gain time, gradually try eroding those time wasters, in favour of what you see as more important. Shift the time allocation over a period of weeks, or a term. Do not try it overnight. You will be ragged by the end of a week.

Changing the way children spend time   How can you increase children's time on task? Examine the list of rules you compiled in the exercise above. Change, in discussion with the children, some of those rules. Monitor the effect of these changes. Progressively develop a set of rules which support time on task rather than break children's application and concentration.

Changing timetabling   Try out some of the ideas in Chapter 3 for the grouping of subjects. Look at a timetable based upon groups of children rather than the whole class. Try building in periods of time where the children can have some control over their use of time.

Groups and groupings

Current groups and groupings

At the heart of good practice is the ability to offer fruitful learning opportunities through the use of groups.

Exercise   List the different sorts of groups you use and the frequency of use of these groupings. Against each grouping put your reasons for the formation of that particular group. Indicate to what extent your grouping arrangements support the following:

Ability	Skills
Friendship	Other criteria developed by you.

Questions

How do you group children in your class? Do you use a planned approach to grouping which is intended to facilitate learning or do you stick to the same groups all of the time?

Does your grouping support learning across the whole curriculum?

What groupings do the children elect to have, and why do you think they group in these ways?

Do you really have groups operating as a team or are they collections of individuals sitting together?

Do you teach children about the nature of groups and group dynamics?

What are your views and experiences concerning leadership in groups?

Action to change groups and groupings

What new forms of grouping can you devise which would be appropriate for special purposes? Try in the first instance to form a group based on complementary skills. To do this you will need to identify a problem in say, science or a mathematical investigation and then put together a group of children who will tackle the problem in different ways and/or offer different skills in, for example, making things, keeping records. Evaluate, with the children, the outcomes of such a group activity. This sort of approach will support your SATs work. Having started to think about groups for specific purposes expand your grouping strategies across the curriculum.

How can you use children's own choice of grouping for learning purposes? Use friendship and other children's choice groups to do two things. Firstly they will provide an excellent starting point for the development of children's self-evaluation. Secondly they will offer you the opportunity to teach the children about teamwork, the characteristics of groups and leadership.

Questions and questioning

Current ways of framing questions and questioning

At the core of learning through groups is the ability of teachers to ask the 'right' question at the 'right' time, and of the 'right' person. Questioning is a sophisticated business. Good questioning is associated with good listening. It is important to bear in mind that research indicates that boys get more attention than girls in questioning sessions. The boys are not only specifically asked more questions, they also get more chances to answer.

Exercise   Find out what sorts of questions you ask the children. Use an audio cassette or ask a colleague to sit in, observe and write them down. You have to do two things with the data; look at the type of questions in terms of the sorts of answers you might get, and to whom you directed your questions. For example, what proportion are open-ended where the child has to work out what to say and how many are closed, where a one word answer (perhaps 'yes' or 'no') is expected? How many are quite specific to one aspect of the task in hand, and how many are exploratory, that is with an infinite range of answers provoked by the child's own thinking? Finally, are you directing questions equally or are some children getting more attention or pressure?

Questions

What sort of a questioner are you?

Is the balance of question type, length, and direction good in relation to the sorts of responses you want to encourage?

Do you give sufficient time for answers?

Do you recognise the possibility that, in the heat of the moment you sometimes reject 'wrong' answers when, in fact, they were only unexpected and were actually good answers?

Do you find follow-up questions easy to handle?

Do you use different sorts of questions with individuals, groups, the class?

Action to change questions and questioning

Good questioners:

> stimulate
> follow the development of ideas
> allow time for answering
> don't discriminate.

Deliberately shift your questioning to include the pluses mentioned above.

To help with this make the periodic use of audio cassettes part of your normal practice. Work with the children on their questioning. Not only will this support their development in relation to English AT1, speaking and listening, but you will also be able to develop your own abilities alongside the children.

Look at the sorts of questions offered in texts, schemes and workcards. Analyse children's mistakes in relation to the question types. This will help you with your questioning and help you understand some of the causes of the children's problems.

Evaluation and assessment

Current evaluation and assessment

Exercise How do you evaluate your own performance? List all the ways in which you collect information about your classroom and yourself. Look at Chapter 8 to see whether there are further ways of collecting information which you might be able to use.

Exercise List the ways you use for testing children's understanding, skills development and concept development.

Questions

What is there about your own performance as a teacher that you would most like to change?

What do you need to find out about your performance in order to work out how to change it?

What are the aspects of your classroom management which will have to change with the introduction of the National Curriculum?

What are the strengths and weaknesses of your assessment and testing approaches? What else do you need to know that these tests don't tell you?

How do you continuously assess? What do you wish to continuously assess?

Action to change evaluation and assessment

Focusing evaluation   Look very carefully at Chapter 8. Are you gathering all of the information you need? If not work out how to collect that information in a way that you can manage. To start this process take a part of your curriculum and plan one or two sessions in terms of the outcomes you would expect. This means that you will have to work out, in advance, how you will evaluate and assess the intended, and possibly unintended, outcomes. As you gain experience expand this approach across the curriculum.

Changing assessment of learning   What devices can you construct which will make it possible to assess children while working with them? How else can you structure your assessment processes to make them manageable? Try evaluating group work with the children. List the problems and possibilities. Can you distinguish between children with a good spoken vocabulary but a lack of understanding in, say, science and children who understand the concept but find it difficult to express that understanding orally?

Summary

In this chapter we have focused on those dimensions which we believe to be at the heart of good classroom practice. We are not suggesting that these are the only ways of examining your practice, but that they are particularly fruitful starting points.

If you attempt the exercises and answer the questions we have posed, you will find that changes take place which will support your introduction of the National Curriculum and the prescribed assessment arrangements.

It is possible to produce models of kinds of school organisation and draw out their strengths and weaknesses. However it is a very complex business and many important factors have to be drawn together. That is beyond the scope of this book. Suffice to say that, in devising whole-school plans, just as in class plans, you need to start from where you are now! It is important to be as objective as you can about the current management and organisation of the school. Decide what the strengths and weaknesses in whole-school strategies are.

Both the good points and those that need attention will, in part, be a reflection of your own style of leadership. To take the school forward into the 1990s you will need to demonstrate clear positive thinking and action, actual not just apparent delegation, the flexibility to adopt leadership strategies appropriate in different situations and stamina to carry through change. Then you can focus on each of the main areas for concern and really 'set the pace'. The important issues are these:

> Planning
> Time management
> Class composition and teaching staff deployment
> INSET
> Communication
> Evaluation.

A review of the situation now, with regard to each of these areas, is the starting point for devising and initiating changes, in order to better cope with National Curriculum demands.

Planning

Current planning

Chapter 7 will help you with current planning. What distinguishes your vision from that of the classteacher is that it views the school as a whole, and can span a longer period of time.

Exercise   Write down the present situation in terms of the sorts of plans that are being produced in the school. Include your own, teachers', support staff's and governors' plans.

Questions

What plans are being implemented right now?

What changes need to be made to these plans to help with National Curriculum implementation?

What things need planning for, that have not received much attention in the past?

To what extent are the plans of all colleagues and governors compatible?

Action to change planning

Remember that it is often the case that whilst individual plans are well thought out and presented they may actually disadvantage some aspects of the whole-school plan.

If there is no school five-year plan write one now, with the help of your staff. Use Chapter 7 to help you do this.

Set up a system for evaluation of the implementation of plans ensuring that the information collected can be used to refine and further develop these.

Be active not reactive with planning. Do not let the National Curriculum reach the children without you yourself and all your staff mastering its implications first.

Time management

Current time management

One of your biggest priorities is to give your staff and the children in the school the maximum opportunity to teach and learn.

Exercise   Find out where your time goes, by keeping a diary for a while. For example, list the following each day:

> How many phone calls?
> Requests, and what for?
> Contacts with parents of prospective pupils?
> Contacts with parents of children in the school?
> Contacts with governors, and about what?
> Time spent on INSET, planning, organising and implementing?
> Contacts with advisors, LEA etc.

Questions

Is playtime or dinner time allowed to overrun?

Are staff waylaid for minor reasons, in the course of the day?

Are children used to take messages or do jobs, without justification?

Are colleagues delegating things to you which they should really take on themselves?

Action to change time management

There are many things you can change but it is a good policy to change only one area at a time.

Start by looking at the fixed points of the school day. What are the constraints of these? Can they be adjusted to give more time on task without losing the sense of community?

Link your consideration of time management with communication around the school.

Plan visits and visiting speakers etc. in relation to the whole curriculum continuity and progression of the school. This should be done as a staff team exercise.

Class composition and teaching staff deployment

Current class composition and teaching staff deployment

Now is the time for a reappraisal of how well the school is matching the skills of the staff to the needs of the children.

Exercise   Find out by consulting their CVs, and asking staff themselves, what their skills are. Find out too what their plans are for their own development.

Questions

Are your classes age based, vertically grouped or what? Why? What is your admissions policy and how does this affect organisation of classes for older children?

Does class organisation permit full access to the whole curriculum for all children?

Are there talents that you and your colleagues have that are not being tapped? If so how could you release this potential?

Action to change class composition and staff deployment

Staff   As far as possible, place staff to exploit their skills and further their own development.

Get staff to share expertise by setting up teams with powers of decision-making and control over timetabling, children's groupings and resources.

Use what you have discovered about your colleagues to inform INSET development.

Changes to class composition   When assessing the children's needs, you will be guided by the views of governors, parents and the staff. All of these people can be won round to the most adventurous and forward thinking of class plans if you can persuade them wholeheartedly that it is in the children's best interests.

Compose classes in a way which you and your staff favour, and which matches the children's needs best. It will then be successful and the children and teachers will all gain. Do not fear, the parents will 'buy' it. After all they have accepted the National Curriculum without noticeable protest, and that represents a schooling revolution. But do pre-empt parental criticism by keeping parents well informed about what is happening in school.

INSET

Current INSET

With the changes made over the last few years your INSET arrangements will have become much more school-based and focused. However, it is important to maintain a balance between activities that have short and long term benefits. Busy teachers are inclined towards practical, short term INSET. But National Curriculum and assessment arrangements will reinforce the need for INSET which also offers change and longer term development opportunities.

Exercise   Give a questionnaire (or ask the staff member having responsibility for INSET) to find out the following information from each member of staff:

> All courses attended over last five years
> The most popular types of courses with reasons
> INSET wishes
> Views of school needs in order of priority.

Questions

In view of the desires and perceived priorities of yourself and staff what is the agenda for action?

What sort of budget can you command? How can this be increased or enhanced? For example, staff expertise, governors, local HE, local business, sharing with other schools are some of the things to explore.

Can you engage staff in the sort of teamwork which will bring about on-the-job development and/or some staff release time?

Action on INSET arrangements

There are suggestions in Chapter 7 about this.

The biggest boost to their own development needs that classteachers can have is some non-contact time. Help to support your staff in team meetings, on courses and visiting other schools by taking their classes. (This includes planning the class work programme for the day and assessing it at the end.)

Plan the INSET programme for the year that:

> helps to meet the children's needs
> helps to meet the whole school needs
> gives the staff opportunities for self-development.

Set up a database of INSET undertaken by your staff. If possible liaise with other heads to see if you can share databases and thus expertise. LEA advisers and local HE institutions can be useful partners.

Communication

Current communication

Exercise   Look carefully at your internal communication system. Do this by getting your secretary to list the communication problems he or she has. Ask colleagues, both teaching and non-teaching, in which areas they find it difficult to get information.

Exercise   Walk around the outside and inside of the school asking yourself what help you would need to find your way if you were a visitor.

Questions

How do colleagues get information about such things as INSET courses?

What access do colleagues have to a telephone?

What information can be given over the telephone by your secretary without bringing in you or your colleagues? Do you need a training opportunity for your secretary to handle this?

How much time is taken using children to deliver messages? Are there other ways of handling this? Is your message really necessary?

Can you use word processing for school documents which may need only minor alterations each year?

What is the quality of paperwork within the school and going to parents?

Action to change communication management

What modifications could be made to make informal communication:

> quicker
> easier
> more efficient?

What improvements can be made to the formal communication system? Chapter 7 will help with this.

Look at how you might use information technology to store data and permit rapid access to information.

Evaluation

Current evaluation

Exercise   Use a staff meeting to generate the strengths and weaknesses of the school's evaluation approaches. Use one of the group discussion techniques in Chapter 8.

Questions

What are current whole-school evaluations like?

What areas do you need to strengthen in terms of obtaining appropriate information?

What are the constraints on action arising from evaluations?

How do the school evaluations inform the school development plan?

What roles does the governing body have? Is it fulfilling that role? Is training or further training needed?

Was a resources inventory compiled recently? Establish what redundant resources the school has, so that they may be offered to other schools or disposed of.

Action to change whole-school evaluation

Ask curriculum consultants to plan and implement whole-school evaluations regarding readiness for National Curriculum delivery. This evaluation would look at teaching skills and resources. These can then feature prominently in the whole-school development plan.

Compile a list of the shortfall in teaching skills and resources. Prioritise the needs and develop solutions, as finance and other conditions permit.

Explore the possibility of staff exchanges and short secondments for the purposes of bringing back new skills and insights.

Summary

We believe that the areas we have focused on in this chapter are those which will offer you the best opportunities for the development of an action plan. Underpinning all of these areas is the clear need for you to offer strong but supportive leadership.

It is a pity that the introduction of something as revolutionary as a National Curriculum should have come at the behest of politicians. They do not have the same vision of education as do teachers. While the picture presented by either is only partial, many teachers do know more about the needs of children. Education is not about going through hoops and over hurdles, it is about the lifelong enrichment of whole people. It is up to you to combine your humanitarianism with your skills as an educationalist to ensure that this continues to be so. We hope this book will help you.

Bibliography

BENNETT, N et al., *Teaching Styles and Pupil Progress* (Open Books, 1976)

CLIFT, P. *et al.*, *Record Keeping in Primary Schools* (Macmillan, 1981)

DES and the Welsh Office (HMSO):

Mathematics for Ages 5 to 16. Proposals of the Secretary of State for Education and Science and the Secretary of State for Wales (1988)

Science for Ages 5 to 16. Proposals of the Secretary of State for Education and Science and the Secretary of State for Wales (1988)

English for Ages 5 to 11. Proposals of the Secretary of State for Education and Science and the Secretary of State for Wales (1988)

Circular No: 6/89 The Education Reform Act 1988: National Curriculum: Mathematics and Science Orders Under Sections 4

DES *National Curriculum: from Policy to Practice* (HMSO, 1989)

GALTON, M *et al.*, *Inside the Primary Classroom* (Routledge and Kegan Paul, 1980)

HARRIS, A. *et al.*, *Curriculum Innovation* (Croom Helm, 1975)

We have referred to and used the Statutory Orders relating to English in the National Curriculum, mathematics in the National Curriculum and science in the National Curriculum, throughout the book, but particularly in Section B and in the creation of some of the figures in Chapters 2, 3 and 10.

Keyword index